Also by Tom Cooper:
A@W Great Lakes Holocaust: The First
Congo War, 1966–1997
A@W Great Lakes Conflagration: The
Second Congo War, 1998–2003
A@W Wings over Ogaden: the Ethiopian–
Somali War, 1978–1979
A@W Libyan Air Wars: Part 1: 1973–1985
A@W Libyan Air Wars Part 2: 1985–1986
A@W Wars and Insurgencies of Uganda,
1971–1993
ME@W Syrian Conflagration, 2011–2013

Also by Adrien Fontanellaz:
A@W Wars and Insurgencies of Uganda,
1971–1993

Published by
Helion & Company Limited
26 Willow Road, Solihull, West Midlands,
B91 1UE, England
Tel. 0121 705 3393
Fax 0121 711 4075
Email: info@helion.co.uk
Website: www.helion.co.uk
Twitter: @helionbooks
Visit our blog http://blog.helion.co.uk/

Designed and typeset by Kerrin Cocks,
SA Publishing Services
kerrincocks@gmail.com
Cover design by Paul Hewitt,
Battlefield Design
www.battlefield-design.co.uk
Printed by Henry Ling Ltd, Dorchester,
Dorset

Text © Tom Cooper & Adrien Fontanellaz,
2015
Monochrome images sourced by the authors
Colour profiles © Tom Cooper, 2015

Cover: Column of RPA insurgents during
advance on Kigali, in April 1994. (Albert
Grandolini Collection)

ISBN 978-1-910294-56-7

British Library Cataloguing-in-Publication
Data.
A catalogue record for this book is available
from the British Library.

For details of other military history titles
published by Helion & Company
Limited contact the above address, or visit
our website: http://www.helion.co.uk.
We always welcome receiving book
proposals from prospective authors.

CONTENTS

GLOSSARY

AB.	Agusta-Bell (Italian helicopter manufacturer)
AC	*Artillerie de Campagne* (field artillery)
AdA	*Armée de l'Air* (French Air Force)
AK	*Avtomat Kalashnikova* (Kalashnikov assault rifle)
AML	*Automitrailleuse Légère* (wheeled armoured vehicle manufactured by Panhard)
APC	Appointed Platoon Commander (sub-lieutenant in the NRA and the RPA)
APC	armoured personnel carrier
ASCC	Air Standardisation Coordinating Committee (US, UK, Australian and New Zealand committee for standardisation of designations for foreign [primarily Soviet] armament; its standardisation codenames are usually known as 'NATO designations')
ATGM	anti-tank guided missile
BAe	British Aerospace, later BAE Systems
Brig Gen	brigadier general
CAP	combat air patrol
Capt	captain
CAS	close air support
CDR	*Coalition pour la Défense de la République* (Coalition for the Defence of the Republic)
CHC	Chairman of High Command
C-in-C	commander-in-chief
CMF	Combined Mobile Force
CND	*Conseil National pour le Développement* (National Council for Development)
CO	commanding officer
COIN	counter-insurgent or counter-insurgency
Col	colonel
CoS	Chief of Staff
COS	*Commandement des operations spéciales* (Special Operations Command)
CPA	*Commando Parachutiste de l'Air* (Air Parachute Commando)
CRAP	*Commando de Recherche et d'Action en Profondeur* (Long-Range Reconnaissance Commando)
DAMI	*Détachment d'Assistance Militaire et d'Instruction* (Military Training and Assistance Detachment)
DBLE	*Demi-Brigade de la Légion Étrangère* (Half-Brigade of the Foreign Legion)
DMI	Directorate of Military Intelligence
DMZ	De-militarised Zone
DP	Democratic Party (of Uganda)
DRC	Democratic Republic of the Congo (Congo-Kinshasa)
DSP	*Division Spéciale Présidentielle* (Presidential Special Division in Zaïre)
ESM	*École Supérieure Militaire* (Higher Military School, military academy in Kigali)
ESO	*École des Sous-Officiers* (NCO School in Rwanda)
FAL	*Fusil Automatique Léger* (light automatic rifle, Belgian-designed firearm)
FAR	*Forces Armées Rwandaises* (Rwandan Armed Forces)
FAZ	*Forces Armées Zaïroises* (Zairian Armed Forces)
FLN	*Front de Libération National* (National Liberation Front, main group of armed opposition during the Algerian War of Independence)
FRELIMO	*Frente de Libertação de Moçambique* (Liberation Front of Mozambique, armed opposition to Portuguese rule in Mozambique, in 1960-1975; later the ruling party in Mozambique)
FRONASA	Front of National Salvation (armed opposition in Uganda, 1971-1979)
GCI	ground controlled interception
Gen	general
GIGN	*Groupe d'Intervention de la Gendarmerie Nationale* (National Gendarmerie Intervention Group, France)
GSIGN	*Groupement de Sécurite et d'Intervention de la Gendarmerie Nationale* (National Gendarmerie Intervention and Security Group, France)
GSIGP	*Groupe de Sécurité et d'Intervention de la Garde Présidentielle* (Presidential Guard Security and Intervention Group, Rwanda)
GSU	General Service Unit
HQ	headquarters
IAP	international airport
IP	instructor pilot
JO1	Junior Officer One (captain in the NRA and the RPA)
JO2	Junior Officer Two (lieutenant in the NRA and the RPA)
KIA	killed in action
Km	kilometre
JUNAR	*Jeunesses de l'UNAR* (UNAR's youth)
KY Kabaka Yekka	(Kings Only Party, Bugandan royalist movement in Uganda)
LRA	Lord's Resistance Army (armed opposition group in south-western Sudan and northern Uganda)
Lt	Lieutenant
Lt Col	lieutenant colonel
MAG	*Mitrailleuse d'Appui Général* (general-purpose machine gun, Belgian-designed firearm)
Maj	major
Maj Gen	major general
MANPADS	man-portable air defence system(s) — light surface-to-air missiles that can be carried and deployed in combat by a single soldier
MBT	main battle tank
MDR	*Mouvement Démocratique Républicain* (Republican Democratic Movement, Rwanda)
MHC	Member of High Command (colonel in the NRA and RPA)
Mi	Mil (Soviet/Russian helicopter designer and manufacturer)
MIA	missing in action
MNC	*Mouvement National Congolais* (Congolese National Movement)

MPR	*Mouvement Populaire Rwandais* (Rwandan Popular Movement)	**RIMa**	*Régiment d'Infanterie de Marine* (Marine Infantry Regiment)
MRL	multiple rocket launcher	**RPA**	Rwandan Patriotic Army (armed opposition group in Rwanda, 1990-1994)
MRLS	multiple rocket launcher system		
MRND	*Mouvement Révolutionnaire National pour le Développement* (National Revolutionary Movement for Development)	**RPF**	Rwanda Patriotic Front (political wing of armed opposition group in Rwanda and political party ruling Rwanda since 1994)
NCO	non-commissioned officer	**RPG**	rocket-propelled grenade
NRA	National Resistance Army (armed opposition in Uganda, 1980-1986 and official title of Ugandan military, 1986-1995)	**SA-3 Goa**	ASCC codename for S-125 Neva/Pechora, Soviet radar-homing surface-to-air system
		SA-7 Grail	ASCC codename for 9K32 Strela-2, Soviet MANPADS
NRM	National Resistance Movement (umbrella political organisation ruling Uganda since 1986)	**SA-16**	ASCC codename for 9K310 Igla-12, Soviet MANPADS
OAU	Organisation of African Unity	**SARM**	*Service d'Action et de Renseignement Militaire* (Military Action and Intelligence Service, Zaïre)
P/JO2	Provisional Junior Officer Two (sub-lieutenant in the NRA and the RPA)		
PARMEHUTU	*Parti du Movement et de l'Émancipation Hutu* (Party of Hutu Movement and Emancipation)	**SAM**	surface-to-air missile
		SHA	Secure Humanitarian Area
PC	Political Commissar	**SIGINT**	Signals Intelligence
PDC	*Parti Démocratique Chrétien* (Christian-Democratic Party, Rwanda)	**SO**	Senior Officer (lieutenant colonel or major in the NRA)
PL	*Parti Libéral* (Liberal Party, Rwanda)	**UFF**	Uganda Freedom Fighters
PRC	People's Republic of China	**UFM**	Uganda Freedom Movement
POW	prisoner of war	**UK**	United Kingdom
PRM/PRA	Popular Resistance Movement/Popular Resistance Army	**UN**	United Nations
		UNC	Uganda National Congress
PSD	*Parti Social-Démocrate* (Social-Democratic Party, Rwanda)	**UNLA**	Uganda National Liberation Army (armed opposition group in Uganda, 1979-1980)
PSU	Public Safety Bureau	**UNRF**	Uganda National Rescue Front
RAMa	*Régiment d'Artillerie de Marine* (Marine Artillery Regiment)	**UPC**	Uganda People's Congress
		UPM	Uganda Patriotic Movement
RDP	*Régiment de Dragons Parachutistes* (Parachutist Dragoons Regiment)	**US$**	United States Dollar
REI	*Régiment Étranger d'Infanterie* (Foreign Infantry Regiment)	**USSR**	Union of Soviet Socialist Republics (or Soviet Union)
REP	*Régiment Étranger de Parachutistes* (Foreign Parachute Regiment)	**VIP**	very important person
		WIA	wounded in action
RICM	*Régiment d'Infanterie Chars de Marine* (Marine Infantry Tank Regiment)		

CHAPTER ONE:
INTRODUCTION

This is the second of two volumes that are providing a history of inter-related military conflicts in Uganda and Rwanda that were raging from 1960s well into the 1990s. While it is safe to say that majority of African conflicts tend to attract very limited attention of the public in the West, this was clearly not the case for Rwanda of 1994, when a three-years-long civil war culminated in a genocide that nearly eliminated the Rwandan Tutsi community and radically changed the political landscape of the country. More than 20 years later hundreds – if not thousands – of scientific works have been published about tragic events that occurred in 1994, and that is without mentioning earlier reports, articles, and books. Theoretically, most aspects of this

part of that country's history – like internal politics, involvement of the UN and various foreign powers – are relatively well-researched and documented.

Paradoxically, military aspects of the civil war in Rwanda of 1990-1994 – the very topic of this volume – remain poorly covered. At best, data about specific operations, units and people involved are scattered in a myriad of published sources. Precisely this was the impulse that prompted the work on this project. Namely, during the work on books *Great Lakes Holocaust* (Africa@War Volume 13) and *Great Lakes Conflagration* (Africa@War Volume 14), it transpired that this conflict was interconnected with earlier wars in Uganda and in Rwanda, and

The mountains of Rwanda, as seen on an officially-released postcard from the 1970s. (Mark Lepko Collection)

A typical settlement of cattle-herders in Rwanda of the early 20th Century. (Mark Lepko Collection)

that there is a need for a closer study of related military operations, experiences, and relations between leading personalities in Uganda, Rwanda and Zaïre/Democratic Republic of the Congo. Related work resulted in this account, which is attempting to dissect and summarise the military history of the Rwandan Civil War between October 1990 and August 1994, with special emphasis on coverage of coming into being of the Rwandan Patriotic Front.

Of course, military operations are never happening in a vacuum but are a part of a wider context, and therefore we decided to add descriptions of geopolitical circumstances as necessary. Although these are kept to an absolute minimum and used solely to explain the backgrounds for specific developments, the reader should be forewarned that this account is no attempt to provide a 'full spectrum' history of Rwandan tragedy. Rwandan Patriotic Front, 1990-1994, is merely a complement to the numerous and authoritative – but not focused on military – works already published.

In slightly different practice than usually in our works of this kind, research for this book is based on primary documents, numerous scientific studies, and reputable publications, and rather few interviews with participants and eyewitnesses. This results in what might appear as rather 'intensive' use of endnotes: that was necessary because history as a science progresses by peer-reviewing. One author has to allow others that are – or are going to – study the same subject, to have a clear indication of the origin of the information used in the work in order to either agree with and build on them, or disagree, or relativise them according to own perspectives. Of course, we had to take into consideration other factors as well, foremost the requirement for this book to remains 'reader-friendly'. Therefore, we decided not to add notes for publications consulted during our work that we consider – to the best of our knowledge – for 'generally accepted'. On the other hand, we have systematically provided sources whenever our own conclusions differ from relative – or at least 'partially mainstream' – historiography.

Some of titles listed in Bibliography might appear 'controversial' to well-informed readers. Through our research and travels, the authors are uncomfortably familiar with the many bloody wars fought in Africa over the last 50 years. We consider any source to be relevant until it can be proven beyond doubt to be without merit. It is a matter of fact that governments, national and private organisations, private companies and certain individuals face harsh ramifications when their influence and/or participation in such conflicts become public.

The authors therefore carefully collected all the available information, cross-examined various sources, correcting and updating their findings with the aim of offering the most detailed and dependable insight possible, with the objective of providing a comprehensive set of answers to questions like who, when, where, how and why. Furthermore, we have gone to great lengths in order to 'depoliticise' the manuscript. This meant avoiding the use of terms such as 'regime', 'rebels', 'terror' or 'terrorist'. Clearly, one man's 'freedom fighter' is another's 'terrorist'. Reason is that having no political axe to grind, we have instead concentrated on recording and describing the military history of Rwanda, and have thus made all efforts to maintain a non-partisan narrative that remains readable and easy to understand.

For similar reasons, but also in order to simplify the use of this book, all names, locations and geographic designations are as provided in *The Times World Atlas*, or other traditionally accepted major sources of reference.

Land of the Thousand Hills

Rwanda is a small country landlocked in Central Africa. With 26.338 square kilometres (10.169 square miles), it is smaller than the Federal State of Maryland in the USA, or the Former Yugoslav Republic of Macedonia in southern Europe. It borders to Uganda in the north, Tanzania in the East, Burundi in the South and the Democratic Republic of the Congo (DRC) in the West.

Most of Rwanda lies at altitudes over 1,000 metres (3.280ft) above the sea surface. Central portion is dominated by a hilly plateau averaging about 1,700m (5,600ft) in elevation that gave it the nick-name 'The Land of the Thousand Hills'. Eastward, the land slopes downward to a series of marshy lakes along the upper Kagera River. On the western side is a mountain system averaging about 2,740m (about 9,000ft), forming the watershed between the Nile and Congo river systems. The Virunga Mountains, a volcanic range that forms the northern reaches, includes Vulcan Karisimbi (4,507m/14,787ft), Rwanda's highest peak. West of the mountains the elevation drops to about 1,460m (about 4,800ft) in the Lake Kivu region.

The climate is generally mild with an average annual temperature of 18°C, but there are wide temperature variations because of elevation differences. Indeed, in the mountains of the northwest frost occurs at night through all of the year. Rwanda has three main seasons: a short dry season in January, the major rainy season from February through May, and another dry period from May until October. The

A parade of the Royal Guard during the occupation of German East-Afrika by Belgians, in 1916 or 1917. (Mark Lepko Collection)

A panoramic view of Kigali and the hills surrounding the city. (Adrien Fontanellaz Collection)

yearly rainfall is heaviest in the western and north-western mountain regions.

Rwanda used to be covered by extensive forests of eucalyptus, acacia, and oil palms, but forests now cover over only about 12.5% of the land and are concentrated in the western mountains and Lake Kivu area. Because Rwandans traditionally rely on firewood for up to 90% of their energy, the country's forests have been preserved through reforestation efforts, and overall 14.7% of Rwanda is designated as protected area. Wildlife is including elephant, hippopotamus, crocodile, wild boar, leopard, antelope, and flying lemur – and is protected in Akagera National Park. The Virunga Mountains are the home of famous mountain gorillas.

Traditional Rwandan economy was subsistence economy. Hoe is still used as the main tool, and the main cash crop is coffee, with amounts of tea and pyrethrum produced too. Because of intensive agriculture, the country not only suffers from soil erosion and occasional droughts, but lacks major mineral resources too, although mines used to be Rwanda's second most important source of foreign exchange (after agricultural products) in the 1960s-1980s period. Namely, while there is some cassiterite (tin ore), wolframite (tungsten ore), columbite and there are reports about large natural gas reserves near the border to the Democratic Republic of the Congo (DRC), due to drops in world commodity prices the mining of cassiterite was halted in 1986. The following year the country's wolframite mines were closed for the same reason. Some exploitation was re-started in 1991, but only in very modest amounts: political instability has caused frequent disruptions in trade and decline in exports, leading ever more people to revert to subsistence agriculture, in turn increasing environmental problems.

Because of its hospitable climate – more favourable for agriculture than in neighbouring countries – Rwanda is one of most densely populated countries in Africa. The land is intensively farmed: as of 1990, about 92% of the Rwandan workforce used to be involved in agriculture, which in turn resulted in deforestation, exhausting and overgrazing, and even to desertification throughout the country.

As of 1990, three ethnic groups made up the population: the Hutu (about 86%); the Tutsi (14%); the Twa (1%), and pygmoid people thought to be the original inhabitants of the region. Most of the people live in family groups housed in grass huts in farms scattered over country's many hills, but majority are concentrated in the south. Traditionally, the principal goal in life was parenthood. About half the population

was Roman Catholic, 39.4% Protestant (including 12.2% Adventist and 27.2% other Protestant), 4.5% other Christians, 1.8% Muslim, while the remainder of the people follow traditional religions. The official languages were Kynarwanda (a Bantu language) and French. Schooling was free and compulsory for children aged 7 through 13, but only about 80% of the adult population was literate. The civil war of 1990-1994 greatly disrupted the ethnic and geographic distribution of the population and caused massive numbers of deaths, although the density of population remains high.

Rwanda was divided into 12 prefectures (administrative structure has significantly changed since 1994), each of which was administered by a prefect appointed by the president. Prefectures were further divided into districts and municipalities. Principal cities were Kigali (the capital) and Butare (former colonial capitol). The country had a relatively good road network of 12,000km (7,456miles) but only a small portion of this was paved as of 1990. There used to be no railroad, although Rwanda was linked to the Uganda-Kenya railroad system: majority of Rwanda's international trade passed through the Kenyan port of Mombasa. The main international airport was Grégoire Kayibanda International Airport (IAP), outside Kigali (re-named since 1994).

Early History of Rwanda

Despite hospitable climate and intensive agriculture, centralised political entities appeared only relatively late in Rwanda. The first known inhabitants were the Twa, while the Hutu – probably from the Congo Basin – established themselves in the area only by the 15th Century, when the Tutsi came down from the north and partially settled in the area. According to popular mythology, the highlands of what are today Rwanda and Burundi were feudal kingdoms where the Tutsi aristocracy ruled over masses of the Hutus. Correspondingly, the Tutsi attempted to enforce the Hutu into a caste of subjugated and economically dependant serfs. This in turn gave birth to the Hutu ideology that the Tutsi must be resisted at all cost. Although the Tutsi eventually established themselves in the Buganza area by the end of the 17th Century, and expanded their kingdom during the 18th Century, when Germans arrived in the area in the mid-19th Century they found Tutsi King Rwabugili struggling with a predominantly Hutu population. A 'centraliser', Rwabugili actually ruthlessly tamed lineages between Tutsi and Hutu, imposing 'the crown' above all other issues. He was launching unsuccessful campaigns against the

Tutsi refugees – foremost orphans – in southern Uganda, February 1964. Known as '59ers', many of them were to play a crucial role in the future of several Central African countries. This is a view of Entebbe, with Lake Victoria in the background, as of 1910.
(Mark Lepko Collection)

The last King of Rwanda, Kigeli V Ndahindurwa (or Jean-Baptiste Ndahindurwa), ruled his country for only nine months before being forced into exile. (Mark Lepko Collection)

territories that are now part of Uganda, Burundi and the DRC, and never gained effective control over most of them. Not only that several Hutu clans in the northern mountains of modern-day Rwanda remained out of his reach, but only one of his successors, King Kigeri IV (who reigned in the last quarter of the 19th Century), was slightly more successful.[1]

However, the history of Hutu-Tutsi conflict should not be entirely seen through the prism of ethnic differences. Namely, while status of individual Rwandans was inherited by birth, there were lots of inter-ethnic-marriages, and the two ethnic groups shared the same territory, language and religion. Before the colonialisation Rwandans foremost identified themselves by their clan – most of which included Hutu and Tutsis alike. The aristocracy was largely – but not exclusively – drawn from the Tutsi population, but most of chiefs of the land were Hutu. This was the situation the first European – John Hanning Speke – found when he visited the area, in 1858, followed by German explorers in 1880s, and missionaries of the Roman Catholic clergy. Indeed, it was the Germans – who administered the future Rwanda and Burundi as the Protectorate of Ruanda-Urundi from 1897 until 1916, and the Belgians who administered Rwanda-Urundi as a mandate territory from 1947 until 1962 – that helped the Tutsi

monarchists assert authority over the Hutus. Namely, while German implantation in Rwanda remained minimal (even as of 1914, only 96 Europeans lived in the country), Germans ruled it through the policy of indirect rule, turning the Tutsi aristocracy into their local agents. Disunited over succession issues, and feeling threatened by the Belgians settling in nearby Kivus (nowadays in the eastern DRC), the Rwandans accepted this policy as a necessary evil. This resulted in a situation where the protectorate was ruled by a mutually beneficial alliance between the foreigners and the royal court.[2]

When the World War I erupted, the King mobilised 2,500 own warriors armed with traditional weapons to reinforce approximately 50 armed Germans supposed to defend Rwanda. Unsurprisingly, the Belgians under General (Gen) Charles Tombeur seized Rwanda relatively easily, forcing the small German contingent to retreat into Tanganyka. With most of the country devastated during the campaign, the King rallied to the victor and paid a huge tribute by mobilizing about 20,000 men serve as carriers for Belgians. Up to two thirds of these never came back: they fell to tropical diseases while in Tanganiyka.[3]

Once in control of Rwanda, Belgians imposed military administration until receiving a mandate to 'administer' the area from the League of Nations. Influenced by racist theories then en vogue in the West, Belgian authorities continued German policies of supporting education by missionaries, ruling through the Tutsi aristocracy – and cementing the second-class-status of the Hutu. Indeed, while failing to understand that majority of the Tutsi were impossible to recognise from their Hutu neighbours after centuries of living together, they saw the Tutsi as natural 'overlords', supposedly 'altogether different and superior'. Tutsi aristocracy benefited from this blunder because they came into a position to grab more land. Obviously, the most devastating consequence of this misreading was that the Rwandans began to follow the suit and started reading their history along racial terms too.[4]

Violent Independence

As political consciousness increased among Africans after the World War II, the Hutu grew more vocal in protesting against political and social inequalities. Combined with problems experienced when members of the Tutsi aristocracy began to express sympathies towards self-determination and independence, this prompted the Belgians to completely reverse their policies, in the 1950s. In 1958, the caste system was disbanded. Nevertheless, antagonism between the Hutu and the Tutsi was then furthered by rival political parties and eventually erupted into riots and violence. On 1 November 1959, a member of the Hutu Movement and Emancipation Party (PARMEHUTU, later renamed the Democratic Republican Movement, MDR-PARMEHUTU) was beaten by supporters of the Rwandan National Union (UNAR), created by conservative and pro-independence Tutsi. The incident triggered a wave of unrest that left more than 300 dead in two weeks, forcing the King together with about 200,000 refugees to flee to Uganda, a year later.[5]

The PARMEHUTU Party won the first local elections, held in mid-1960s, and became the dominant player on the political scene.

Following a referendum held in January 1961, it abolished the monarchy and won legislative elections held in September of the same year, gaining a large majority of the seats in the National Assembly.

Belgium granted independence to Rwanda at the insistence of the United Nations (UN) on 1 July 1962, with Grégoire Kayibanda – leader of the MDR-PARMEHUTU – as president.[6] Although Kayibanda's rule became more and more authoritarian in style, and his base support began to diminish over the time, the MDR-PARMEHUTU won the elections in 1965 and 1969 too but the cycle of violence continued through the 1960s, with leading Tutsis launching insurgencies and murdering Hutus, and Hutus retaliating with large-scale slaughter and repression of the Tutsis. This not only forced additional elite Tutsi to flee to Uganda – where they became known as the '59ers' – and other neighbouring countries, but also prompted the government to introduce a system of quota, limiting the number of Tutsi with access to positions as public servants with 9%.

Kayibanda's political career came to a sudden end on 5 July 1973, when the Chief of Staff (CoS) of the *Forces Armées Rwandaises* (Armed forces of Rwanda, FAR), Juvénal Habyarimana (a Hutu), took power in a military coup d'état that gave birth to the Rwandan 'Second Republic'. Although continuing the discrimination of his political predecessors, the new president did reduce the violence and introduce some degree of economic prosperity. Under Habyarimana's rule the country evolved into a single-party state whose ideology advocated classic catholic values and a focus on economic development through hard work and collective discipline. The relatively well-managed Rwanda thus soon became popular among Western donors and received a significant influx of financial aid from abroad. This proved instrumental not only for stability of the country, but also for steady economic growth until the second half of the 1980s, when the fall of tin, coffee and tea prices on the international markets stroke a heavy blow.

Military Build-up[7]

Origins of the Rwandan military can be traced back to the times of pre-colonial history, when monarchs like Kigeri IV established relatively sophisticated military services. While earlier kings usually raised new armies whenever ascending the throne, and only tended to allocate men and cattle to garrisons in threatened areas as necessary, in Kigeri's system or rule all the men – regardless if Hutu, Tutsi or Twa – were virtually part of the army. After having honed their skills in the use of bows, javelins, shields and swords at dedicated schools, they were drafted for years to serve in units with specific designations. However, while effective for protection from incursions of slave-traders, even such a military service proved hopelessly outclassed by Western military forces that began to appear in the region towards the end of the 19th Century. This reality became plain obvious when a detachment of the Royal Rwandan Army deployed to repulse a Belgian force was devastated during the Battle of Shangi, in July 1896.

Strong impression the Rwandan contingents left while supporting German troops in 1914-1915, resulted in Belgians disbanding the Royal Army in 1916 and replacing it with their own Force Publique (Public Force). Primarily tasked with maintaining law

A view of one of the specially decorated arches set up in Kigali to mark the independence of Rwanda on 1 July 1962. (UN)

President Grégoire Kayibanda (centre, sitting behind the inscription 'Rwanda') with the Rwandan delegation at the UN in New York. (UN)

and order in Rwanda and Burundi, this force remained small and even as of December 1925 included only 7 Belgian officers and non-commissioned officers (NCOs), and 580 Congolese corporals and privates. The King was only allowed to keep a small Royal Guard composed of Twa warriors armed with spears and bows.

Congolese independence of 30 June 1960 forced Belgian authorities to completely reverse their policy. Not only that they deployed units of the metropolitan army to replace the Force Publique, but also began creating a local armed force. Initially, they hoped that Rwanda and Burundi would form a united country, and therefore planned accordingly. However, this perspective soon unravelled and instead they concentrated on organising the Garde territoriale (Territorial Guard) in Rwanda, in second half of 1960.

Re-designated as the *Garde Nationale* (National Guard) on 12 December 1960, the new force was commanded by Maj François-Louis Vanderstraeten and led by 21 other Belgian officers. While organised into only nine platoons and a small reserve based in Kigali, the National Guard had own training facilities including a NCO-School in Butare (opened on 10 October 1960), and an Officer School in Kigali (opened in November 1960).

The Belgian attitude towards the National Guard was ambiguous at first, but they had to provide for the future, independent Rwanda. On the other hand: traumatised by the decay of a similar force in the

DRC, they were reluctant to develop it into a power that could present a threat for own troops that were still in the country. Therefore, the National Guard began receiving firearms only once the Rwandan independence was certain, in October 1961. Nevertheless, in December 1960, seven Rwandan cadets began their 18 months training in Belgium: six of them – including Juvénal Habyarimana and Alexis Kanyarengwe – successfully completed the course and were promoted to the rank of sous-lieutenant (sub-lieutenant) on return to Rwanda, in April 1962, where each took over the command of one of platoons. By late 1961, the National Guard totalled 47 Belgian officers and NCOs, 677 Rwandan soldiers, corporals and NCOs, and was armed with 707 old Lee-Enfield rifles, 46 FAL assault rifles, 66 pistols, 20 trucks, 24 Jeeps and 5 cars.

Congolese troops of the Public Force in the early 1960s. (RDF)

On Rwandan independence, the National Guard received a consignment of materials left behind by the Belgians, including 30 mortars, 97 additional FAL rifles, and 100 different vehicles. Meanwhile enlargened to 15 platoons – divided between an intervention force based in Kigali and few small garrisons – the Belgians considered establishment of this small force a success. Cooperation between Belgian and Rwandan militaries was good, soldiers correctly paid and well-fed, and disciplined. This enabled another decrease of the Belgian contingent – from 49 to 29 – in May 1963: two months later, Habyarimana was promoted in rank to captain and officially took over from Maj Vanderstraeten, although the latter remained in the country to support his successor.

UNAR Insurgency

Little known at the time, the National Guard carried in it a seed of several problems. Not only that almost all its troops were Hutu, but they were primarily Northerners too (considered more suitable for military service by Belgians), and most were only poorly educated. This stood in opposition to the new political leadership of the country, most of whom – including President Kayibanda – were Southerners.

In 1960, majority of the Tutsi political elite in exile began organising itself as the 'UNAR extérieure' (Foreign UNAR). After a period of attempting to gain political support from aboard – primarily from the UN, but also from the Union of Soviet Socialist Republics (USSR, also known as Soviet Union), People's Republic of China (PRC), Ethiopia, Egypt, Morocco, Mali and Liberia – they opted for an armed struggle. Politically divided (some were traditional monarchists while others were motivated by more progressive ideas of African leaders like Patrice Lumumba or Kwame Nkrumah), they also

Belgian police officers from the Public Force, seen while trying to disperse a group of PARMEHUTU demonstrators, in 1959. (RDF)

experienced significant problems with recruitment of potential fighters. UNAR's militants – they called themselves 'Inkotanyi' ('fighters/warriors'), but were dubbed 'Inyenzi' ('cockroaches') by Rwandan authorities and Belgians – were scattered in refugee camps in Burundi, the Congo, Tanzania and Uganda. Together with the rivalry between leading figures, this resulted in no unified chain of command or cohesive strategy.[8]

First incursions of UNAR insurgents into Rwanda began in 1961, and were very limited by scale. Most of the time small gangs managed little else but to target specific Hutu notables, PARMEHUTU, or European civilians, usually by night. The first Belgian citizen was killed on 21 December 1961 and – following few other attacks – five were murdered near Gabiro, on 10 January 1962. A platoon of the National Guard led by a Belgian NCO, attacked an UNAR camp inside Uganda and killed two insurgents in return, few days later. However, when an insurgent attack on 14 April 1962 left behind four victims – including another Belgian – Kigali ordered heavier retribution against the local Tutsi civilians.

During the following weeks, in attempt to disrupt Rwandan economy, the Inkotanyi began to target trucks hauling oil, forcing the National Guard to start regulating traffic and organising truck-convoys. On 23 May 1962, a column of nine trucks was ambushed while moving along the road from Kigali to Uganda, but a squad of Belgian paras that escorted it repulsed the assault and captured one of insurgents.

Major-General Juvénal Habyarimana as seen in 1973. (Mark Lepko Collection)

Juvénal Habyarimana as seen during a visit in the USA, in 1980, in the function of President of Rwanda. (Photo US DoD)

Increasingly vivid activity of insurgents eventually prompted Brussels to launch its first military intervention in Rwanda, by deploying the 4th Commando Battalion, detachments from various other metropolitan units, several North American T-6A Texan light strikers and other aircraft to Bujumbura in Burundi. Their rigorous patrol activity significantly reduced the insurgent freedom of movement already before the Belgians launched the first 'pacification operation'. In three months prior to legislative elections of 25 September 1961, the Belgian and Rwandan military forces killed 171 civilians, primarily Tutsis. The Inkotanyi intensified their operations in October 1961, but Belgians and the National Guard killed 198 – including many 'assumed authors of violence'. By the time of their departure from Rwanda, the Belgian military lost 11 soldiers in that country, mostly killed in different accidents.[9]

The organisation and conduct of operations of the UNAR improved significantly after Rwandan independence and once the Belgians pulled out – partially because insurgents began receiving support from the government of Patrice Lumumba's *Mouvement National Congolais* (Congolese National Movement, MNC) in the DRC. Furthermore, in 1963, King Kigeri V visited China where he allegedly received US$ 120,000 to improve financing of the UNAR, and where ten Inkotanyi should have been trained in tactics of revolutionary warfare. Although left on its own, the National Guard operated effectively and repelled two major insurgent incursions that aimed to reach Gisenyi and Akagera, in July and in September 1962, respectively.

Following another failed incursion attempt, in November 1963 – after which a number of their leaders were caught and hung – the insurgents decided to end the struggle with one, big, coordinated operation. Correspondingly, all of their contingents in Burundi, Congo and Uganda entered Rwanda simultaneously, with the aim of reaching Kigali. On 21 and 22 December 1963, National Guard intercepted the group that entered from the Congo, captured 90 insurgents and summarily executed them. The two groups that entered from Uganda were even less successful: one was stopped already at the border, while the other – totalling up to 600 combatants – was heavily counter-attacked by the National Guard and lost up to half of its fighters dead or injured.

Nevertheless, a group of about 40 insurgents that entered from Burundi managed to assault the military base in Gako that was still under construction, and to rout its garrison, capturing 7 and forcing 29 other troops to flee, on 21 December. The insurgents then marched into the internal refugee camp at Nyamata where they rallied hundreds of volunteers among the Tutsi, most of whom were victims of government's prosecution. Reinforced, they then marched on Kigali until stopped at the Kanzenze Bridge, about 19 kilometres (12 miles) outside the capital, by a platoon of the National Guard led by Belgian officer. The Inkotanyi and their new allies were decimated by machine guns and mortars, and forced to flee back towards the border of Burundi.

Meanwhile, the National Guard mobilised all of its units and launched a pursuit: it retook the Camp Gako, during the same evening and then reached the border, but not before losing two troops to insurgent snipers that did well in slowing down the military's advance. Finally, shortly before re-entering Burundi, the Inkotanyi executed their seven prisoners.

Slaughter[10]

From the standpoint of the government in Kigali, National Guard's operations against Tutsi insurgents were only the first phase of the struggle against Inkotanyi. The second phase was initiated already on 21 December 1963, when about 200 Tutsi and Hutu politicians opposed to the government were arrested, and between 15 and 20 of them summarily executed by the police. Immediately afterwards, several ministers of the government were sent to the southern prefectures to organise pogroms against the Tutsi population. Working in close cooperation with committees of Civilian Self-Defence, local prefects, mayors and PARMEHUTU-activists armed with spears and clubs were let lose through local villages: in a little more over a month, they murdered around 10.000 Tutsi, of whom about 5,000 in the Gikongoro Prefecture alone.

While attracting next to no international attention – in the light of

A rare photograph of FAR Para-Commandos in the process of embarking upon the sole Noratlas transport prior to a training drop in the mid-1980s. (MATAPARA Collection)

the Cold War, and because of their ties to the PRC, Inkotanyi were generally seen as 'communists' – this wave of terror motivated by blind hatred was to play a tremendous role in the future of Rwanda. Not only that prompted another wave of refugees – estimated at 120,000 in late 1963, but increasing to 336,000 by late 1964 (according to the UN) – to flee abroad but it also delivered a precedent for many similar atrocities in the future.

The utter failure of its offensive in December 1963 marked the beginning of the end for the UNAR. Meanwhile severely divided and led by figures that lacking in leadership and organisational skills, it split into different factions. Two of these – the Mouvement Populaire Rwandais (Rwandan Popular Movement, MPR) and the *Jeunesses de l'UNAR* (UNAR's Youth, JUNAR), allied themselves with the Simba insurgents in the DRC. Those that were trained by the Cuban mission led by Ernesto Che Guevara, have shared the failure of that insurrection: when the Congolese military recaptured the Kivus, Rwandan insurgents have lost all of their bases there.

During the following years, something similar happened to the UNAR in Burundi, Uganda and Tanzania. Although predominantly Tutsi, the government of Burundi stopped its policy of tolerating insurgents under increasing international pressure (Burundian police even shot to death one of loading Rwandan Tutsi exiles, Kayitare Masudi). By 1968, governments of Uganda and Tanzania forbade all activity of the UNAR on their territory, resulting in the end of insurgent activity.

Coup of 1973[11]

As mentioned earlier, primary political base of Kayibanda's government – and the major part of the ruling class that came into being during the 1960s – was from southern Rwanda, while majority of troops of the National Guard were Northerners. Unsurprisingly, relations between these two groups gradually degenerated into open antagonism and the president began taking steps to neutralise what he saw a threat to his rule. Through early 1960s, Kayibanda relied

on the National Police for his safety: most of Police-officers were Southerners and their average salary was higher than that of their counterparts serving in the Guard. However, on 26 June 1973, the President decreed the dissolution of the police and its integration into the National Guard. While, at first glance, this decision appeared like improving the position of the Guard, actually it modified the regional composition of its officer corps – because of the massive influx of police officers from southern Rwanda. Therefore, this action tightened Kayibanda's grip on the military while significantly reducing the influence of Northerners.

Not entirely satisfied, the President then decided to re-shuffle some of military officers to positions in civilian administration. For example, a major (Maj.) from the Guard was appointed a manager of a tea factory. Since already the difference in wages of military and police personnel caused quite some frustration, such decision caused growing discontent – also among the population. Attempting to alleviate the growing rifts between the Hutu, Kayabinda then launched a new campaign against the Tutsi – and here his actions were indirectly supported by those of the government of neighbouring Burundi, which launched a campaign of murders of well-educated Hutu, intending to physically destroy any source of future contest. Whether by accident or design, Rwandan president then certainly went too far when, during a public appearance in July 1973 – and apparently upset by malfunction of his microphone – he went on record to challenge his opponents to try overthrowing him if they thought they could do better than him. A military coup d'état was now nearly unavoidable.

Early in the morning of 5 July 1973, Defence Minister and Chief-of-Staff (CoS) of the National Guard, Juvenal Habyarimana deployed the AML-60 armoured cars of the Guard's sole Armoured Squadron – supported by infantry – to arrest and put the president under a house arrest. Meeting no resistance and without any bloodshed, he toppled the government and the next morning announced that a

'Committee for Peace and National Union' has taken over, ending the First Rwandan Republic.

While Habyarimana's coup resulted in no casualties, his subsequent rule did: during the following years at least 55 politicians closely associated with Kayibanda were starved to death in jail. The former president suffered a similar fate in 1978. On the other hand, although the demise of Kayibanda's government had clearly illustrated that – by its very nature – the military was a potential threat for every government, Habyarimana was quite successful in maintaining a tight grip on the National Guard, and largely kept it out of politics.[12]

Reasons for relative success of his government were that while continuing to act the Minister of Defence and the CoS, Habyarimana was ready to share some of his power and responsibilities. Although in the constitutional system of the Second Rwandan Republic the presidential power was nearly absolute (at least in theory), the president carefully balanced positions of various powerful networks in the country – most likely because he did not came from any of powerful clans and, indeed, depended on that of his wife Agathe Habyarimana for political basis. As a result, potential rivals between Northerners split into several rivalling factions, including the group called 'Akazu', which gravitated around the First Lady.

Further divisions were created by the fact that any ambitious man couldn't get promoted without some clientelism and patronage. This had the negative effect in so far that not always the most able candidates were promoted in rank (or at least not as fast as their better-connected comrades), and that many of high-ranking officers served in their position for decades.[13] Similarly, anybody with even distant connections to officers that fell out of favours had his career blocked without ever knowing why, while in other cases, out-casted, incompetent or undisciplined officers were not fired, but relegated to 'secondary' units, such like the Mutara Independent Company.[14]

An indisputably positive effect of Habyarimana's coup was that he immediately ended the prosecution of Tutsi population, although retaining the de-facto apartheid system. Arguably, his other major decision was of dubious nature: through 1972, he reorganised the National Guard as the Armée Rwandaise (Rwandan Army), established the Gendarmerie Rwandaise (Rwandan Gendarmerie) and put both of these under the control of the Ministry of Defence under the aegis of *Forces Armées Rwandaises* (Rwandan Armed Forces, FAR).

Cooperation with Foreign Powers[15]

Despite his military background, Habyarimana did not launch a major expansion of the military after climbing to power: instead, he strictly limited the share of expenses for defence in the national budget. Until 1989, this was among the lowest in all of Africa, making only about 1.53% of the Gross Domestic Product. Indeed, the further expansion was rather gradual and can be described as 'logical under prevailing conditions'. Foremost: it would most likely remain impossible without support from abroad.

During the First Rwandan Republic, Belgium kept a virtual monopoly on military cooperation with the National Guard. Few

A still from a video showing one of the Chinese-made Type-55 twin-barrel anti-aircraft cannons calibre 37mm, operated by the LAA Battalion in position near Grégoire Kayibanda IAP, outside Kigali. (Adrien Fontanellaz Collection)

A still from a video showing a column of VBL (foreground) and AML-90 armoured cars of the Reconnaissance Battalion FAR. While AML-90's low-velocity cannon calibre 90mm was obsolete as an anti-tank weapon in 1990, it was still proving to be devastating against infantry. Because of this, the vehicle remained a primary provide of firepower for the FAR and was deployed in small groups on all of battlefields of the Rwandan Civil War. (Albert Grandolini Collection)

Belgian officers even occupied command positions until 1973, while others played crucial role in the training sector – particularly for the work of the Officer School and the Bigogwe Commando Training Centre. In 1973, the 40 Belgian advisors present in the country were instrumental for establishment of the *École Supérieure Militaire* (Military Academy; ESM). Rwandans enjoyed relatively liberal access to Belgian military academies, while the Kanombe Military Hospital benefited from cooperation with similar Belgian institutions. Subsequently, Brussels began progressively reducing its support – primarily for financial reasons – and the number of advisors decreased to 20 during the 1980s.[16]

In comparison, military cooperation with France was extremely limited. For reasons explained above, Kayibanda was not keen to improve the condition of the National Gard, while the French were unfamiliar with the country and respecting Belgian interests. Because of this, Paris limited its contacts to Kigali to the sale of 12 AML-60 armoured cars and two Aérospatiale SA.316B Alouette III light helicopters at favourable prices, in March and April 1967, respectively.

The coup of 1973, Habyarimana's standpoint of a Francophile,

Belgian need to reduce support it was providing, French interest in establishing themselves as the flagship of French-speaking world, and Rwanda's position on the borders to mineral wealth of Congo/Zaire, combined to change the situation. Already in December 1973, Paris donated a Sud Aviation Caravelle VIP transport for presidential use and two years later a treaty about military cooperation and assistance was signed between France and Rwanda. Even then, the expansion of the FAR was continued at a slow pace. While the flying element of the FAR was reinforced through donation of one Alouette III helicopter in 1977, it was not before 1978 that the Para-Commando Battalion

and the Light Anti-Aircraft (LAA) Battalion came into being. While two additional commando battalions came into being between 1977 and 1980, and several independent territorial platoons were expanded into companies, it was only in 1986 that a relatively large contract for delivery of 17 AML-90 and 16 VBL armoured cars was signed, which enabled expansion of the Armoured Squadron into an Armoured Battalion too.

Meanwhile, and to quite some surprise considering strong pro-West and fiercely anti-Communist stance of Habyarimana's government, Rwanda entered military cooperation with the Democratic People's

A Sud Aviation Caravelle donated by France to Rwanda in December 1973 to serve as transport for President Habyarimana. (Albert Grandolini Collection)

Republic of Korea (North Korea): indeed, it was North Korean equipment – including ZPU-4 quad anti-aircraft machine guns calibre 14.5mm – and advisors that enabled the establishment of the LAA Battalion. Cooperation with Zaire helped the establishment of the Para-Commando Battalion (some members of which were trained at the Airborne Training Centre in N'Djili, near Kinshasa, for three months) and the Ruhengeri Commando Battalion, while Libyans trained the core of the Huye Commando Battalion, established in 1980. Interestingly, the Commanding Officer (CO) of the Para-Commando Battalion in period 1988-1994 was trained in the USA, after a seven-month course at the Algerian Military Security School, while four Rwandan officers also graduated from the US Army Command & General Staff College in Fort Leavenworth. Finally, West Germany provided some training for the National Police before its dissolution, and few German advisers worked with the sole Engineering Company, and the main Trucks & Jeeps Repair Shop of the FAR, until 1994.[17]

The sole Rwandan Noratlas transport operated during the early 1990s was registered 9XR-GY. (Albert Grandolini Collection)

Rwandan Gendarmerie[18]

The military was not the only Rwandan security agency to profit from cooperation with outside powers in the 1970s and 1980s. Right since its inception, the Gendarmerie benefited from cooperation with France and its training and organisation thus soon reflected the one of its French counterpart. Between 1976 and 1978, the French donated – except for typing machines and hand-grenades – also 42 vehicles, 1,350 pistols and 1,000 rifles for its equipment. First group of cadets was trained at the newly-established Gendarmerie School in Ruhengeri and promoted in February 1976, when the first operational group was established in Kigali too. Two other groups followed in 1978, and one in 1980. In 1981, a new workshop constructed with French support opened its doors and became

One of two Britten-Norman BN-2 Islander light transports operated by the Air Squadron FAR in the early 1990s. (Albert Grandolini Collection)

responsible for maintenance of Gendarmerie's vehicles. By 1982, the Gendarmerie totalled 1,441 Gendarmes, including 66 officers. The service was further expanded during following years and by 1989 included 3.017 officers and other ranks.

The reason Habyarimana created the Gendarmerie was to separate issues of defence against outside threats from those related to internal security and law enforcement. The Gendarmerie thus became responsible for general internal security and cooperation with the *Police Communale* (Rural Police), but, in the case of emergency, could be subjected to the control of the military and used for protection of strategic installations.

Overall, the Gendarmerie was organised into the Mobile Reserve based in Kigali, and territorial units dispersed around the country – the largest of which were Groupements (Groups), divided into brigades, companies and platoons. By 1990, each of 12 prefectures in Rwanda had a gendarmerie group, usually based in prefecture-capitol, and by 1993, each of these was about 250 strong in total.

The FAR in 1990[19]

As of 1990, the FAR as a whole was at best comparable with an oversized light infantry brigade.[20] The Army Headquarters (HQ) in Kigali oversaw all the military units and was divided into the usual staff branches, with the G1 Office responsible for administration and personnel matters; G2 for intelligence; G3 for training and operations; and G4 for logistics. There were four major training facilities: all recruits – service was based on voluntary enlistment – underwent basic military training at the Centre d'instruction du Bugesera (Bugesera Training Centre), located in Gako. Officer training was provided by the ESM in Kigali. The Ecole des sous-officiers (Sub-Officers School; ESO) in Butara trained NCOs, while the Bigogwe Commando Training Centre in Gisenyi Prefecture was providing courses to soldiers serving in commando-units and to all the new army officers and NCOs immediately upon their graduation.

Miscellaneous smaller units attached directly to the Army HQ performed a wide range of specific tasks, while (because of the government's 'developmentalist' ideology) all the military units were contributing work to national economic development, prevention of poaching, and provision of health services (included in provision of health services were the Military Hospital in Kigali and a separate Medic Company). The sole Engineer Company of three platoons was providing some support to combat units, while the Base AR (Rwandan Army Base) – organised into five specialised companies (clothing, food, ammunition, transportation and communications) – was responsible for logistics and other services.

Furthermore, the Army HQ exercised control over two minor units: the Military Police Battalion and the Presidential Guards Battalion.[21] Contrary to the situation in many other countries with an authoritarian political system, where presidential-protection units are de-facto an independent armed force, the organic firepower of the Presidential Guard was not superior to that of regular FAR elements, and its companies were actually even smaller. Indeed, neither of the two units had a combat task before 1992.

The mainstay of the FAR fighting power were its commando- and infantry units, generally organised along a classic ternary pattern (for a full order of battle of the FAR as of 1990, see Table 1). Except for their own HQ (including the common S1 to S4 positions), an infantry battalion usually included a services and support company and three infantry companies. The battalion HQ and support companies were equipped with four mortars calibre 81 or 82mm, four heavy machine guns, four recoilless rifles calibre 75mm, and four RPG-7s. Each infantry company included one support and three infantry platoons, each divided in three sections. The support platoons of every company operated three 60mm mortars and three MAG general purpose machine guns. Standard issue rifles were the FAL and the G3.

Early in 1990, the Army operated a total of seven independent infantry companies – named after prefectures where they were based – and three commando battalions. The latter were considered the elite of the FAR: named Huye, Ruhengeri and the Para-Commando Battalion, they were based in Kibungo, Ruhengeri and Kigali, respectively. The Para-Commando Battalion distinguished itself by its parachutist training and this unit included a separate HQ- and a separate Support Company.

Specialised units included the three-platoon-strong Batterie AC (Battery of Field Artillery), equipped with 12 mortars calibre 120mm and the Reconnaissance Battalion. Equipped with at least 33 VBLs, AML-60s and AML-90s, and organised into Squadrons A, B, and C, and one motorised infantry company, the latter was the only armoured unit of the FAR. The Reconnaissance Battalion was never supposed to operate independently but expected to deploy detachments to specific units, as necessary, and serve for reconnaissance- and fire-support-purposes.[22]

Air Power[23]

General lack of resources and threats resulted in the FAR maintaining a comparatively weak air defence component and operating next to no air power as of 1990. The only dedicated air defence unit was the *Battalion d'Artillerie Légère Antiaérienne* (Light Anti-Aircraft Battalion; LAA Battalion), based at the Camp Big Kanombe adjacent to the Grégoire Kayibanda IAP. This position was logical considering strategic importance of this installation and its 3,500 metres (11,483ft) long runway. The only other airport in Rwanda at the time was in Cyangugu, but its 1,500m (4,921ft) long runway was not supported by modern navigational aids. The LAA Battalion was organised into a HQ and Services Battery, and three batteries of anti-aircraft artillery with a total of 27 artillery pieces: two equipped with Type-55, twin-tube flaks calibre 37mm of Chinese origin, and the third with ZPU-4 quadruple machine guns calibre 14.5mm of North Korean origin.

The flying element of the FAR never became independent: the Escadrille d'aviation (Air Squadron) remained under Army HQ, deprived of its own budget and chronically underfunded. Another negative consequence of this dependency was that its highly-qualified and experienced technicians were frequently re-appointed to various ground units, primarily the Recconnaissance Battalion.

Indeed, the Air Squadron existed primarily due to French provision

This SA.365 Dauphin helicopter was used exclusively for VIP transportation purposes. It was last seen in Lanseria, in South Africa, in 1996.
(Albert Grandolini Collection)

One of two AS.350 Ecureuil light helicopters operated by the Air Squadron FAR in the early 1990s. They were primarily used for transporting higher officers around the country, but sometimes also for reconnaissance purposes and for supply missions. (Albert Grandolini Collection)

(the other crashed shortly after delivery, in 1988); two Britten-Norman BN-2A Islanders and an old Nord 2501 Noratlas transport (used for deployment of paras from the Para-Commando Battalion).[24] Furthermore, the Air Squadron operated three Aérospatiale SA.342L Gazelles (out of a pair delivered in 1981, and two others in 1982 and 1984), and two unarmed Aérospatiale AS.350 Ecureuil light liaison helicopters (for a full review of Air Squadron FAR's assets as of 1990, see Table 2). With one of Gazelles armed with a GIAT M621 20mm cannon, and the other two with LM/70/7 launchers for unguided rockets, they represented something like 'main strike force' of the unit. Trained in France during the early 1980s, their pilots were skilled in combat operations by day and night, and knew how to deploy their rockets from ranges out to 1,000 metres in a dive to a very low altitude before taking evasive measures. However, small number of available helicopters limited the opportunity to train additional crews or operate more intensively, although a small group of French advisers ably supported the work of the unit.

Counter-Insurgency Fever

At the eve of the Rwandan Civil War, the FAR was dimensioned and organised as a counter-insurgency force, never prepared for a major war against foreign power of similar capability. As a whole, it was rather a gendarmerie on steroids than a conventional fighting force. The common saying that every military is preparing itself to fight the last war was very much valid for the Rwandan military, because the experience from countering UNAR incursions weighted heavily against development of any other capabilities.

Other reasons for such development of the FAR were deeper-rooted and harder to explain. At the time of inception of the National Guard, its Belgian mentors were influenced by the chaos that followed Congolese independence. This took place at the height of the Cold War, and the Belgians 'instinctively' sought to develop a force capable of countering any 'Communist subversion' – for example attempts from Moscow or Beijing to extend their

of equipment and advisors who taught Rwandans that ground forces need at least limited means of airborne reconnaissance, fire support and liaison capabilities – in addition to providing transportation services for 'very important persons' (VIPs). Except by the Caravelle jet – replaced in 1990 by a single Falcon 50 (civilian registration 9XR-NN) three-engined business-jet – these were provided by a single Aérospatiale SA.365 Dauphin helicopter delivered in October 1981. The Falcon was flown by a crew hired by private company SATIF, contracted by the French government.

By 1990, none of the three Alouette IIIs delivered in 1967 and 1977 was serviceable and the Caravelle was stored too, waiting for a buyer. Nevertheless, the Air Squadron had 17 pilots and 150 other personnel, and still operated eleven aircraft and helicopters – including the Dauphin and the Falcon 50. Other aircraft included one piston-engined Socata R.235 Guerrier light striker, delivered in 1983 sphere of influence. For former colonial powers like Belgium and France, it was essential to protect their dominions against such a threat in order to protect their own economic- and political interests through maintaining friendly governments in power. Hence, from the very beginning, the FAR's main raison d'être was maintenance of internal security.

Furthermore, Rwanda never found itself facing such external threats like – for example – the DRC: Congo – re-named Zaire in 1971 – was a very close ally, while Uganda was torn apart by political violence and near-constant wars. Even tensions with Tutsi-dominated government in Burundi were of limited nature: the two countries were in a state resembling strategic parity, their forces trained and equipped in similar fashion, and France paid attention their governments not to antagonise each other.

Within this context, it is hardly surprising that Rwandan officers received extensive courses in counter-insurgency (COIN) warfare. Most of these taught them about theories developed by French military thinkers like Charles Lacheroy or Roger Trinquier, which came into being during the I Indochina War of the late 1940s and early 1950s. At the time, the French military was confronted with insurgents following doctrine nearly unknown in the West: that of 'revolutionary warfare' or 'popular warfare', along principles developed and defined by Mao Zedong – the leader of the Chinese Communist Party – during its long struggle against the Japanese invaders and Chinese Nationalists, in the 1930s and 1940s.

The first and most important of these lessons was that the control of the population was an absolute pre-requisite for any successful military campaign. Only through establishing such control – with help of provision of necessary manpower and other resources – could an insurgency gradually expand into an effective military force able to oust a government or a foreign occupier. Correspondingly, Mao concluded, such a struggle was impossible to reduce to pure military operations: it was predominantly political by nature.

A few French officers involved in the I Indochina War were quick in understanding the essence and nature of such doctrine and began developing new tactics to counter it. Several of them developed theories about suitable counter-doctrines too, most of which – paradoxically enough – reminded of the doctrine of revolutionary warfare itself.[25] This doctrine spread through the French officer corps and was put to extensive use during the Algerian Liberation War of the late 1950s. Accordingly, French authorities implemented territorial, civilian-military structures to control the population as tightly as possible and deny the insurgents any access to it. The French became pioneers in large-scale use of sophisticated psychological and civil-military operations in the course of Algerian War too: the probably most accomplished example of this doctrine became the Battle of Algiers, during which soldiers of the 10th Paratrooper Division of the French Army successfully eliminated all insurgent networks in the city in a matter of few months.

This 'French School of COIN' was widely exported – particularly to countries in Africa and South America, and was applied by the Belgian military before this country released various of its colonies into independence, too. For example, as early as of 1957, the Public

Force in the DRC conducted a medium-sized military exercise in Katanga code-named 'Operation Tornado' to put related concepts to test and to train COIN warfare. A few years later, when old hands of the Public Force trained the first generation of Rwandan officers, they naturally transmitted this doctrine to the new service: Rwandan officers were thus educated to consider military operations within the context of a wider, political struggle where the real gravity centre was the population. Seeing that quelling an insurgency necessitated a very close cooperation and coordination between local civilian and military hierarchies, and a 'liberal use' of para-military structures to support the regular military, they concluded that their success against the UNAR was primarily a result of a 'sacred union' of the Hutu. Corresponding lessons were to be applied in any similar war in the future.

Table 1: Main Combat Units of the FAR, 1 October 1990

Unit	CO	
Presidential Guard Battalion	Maj Léonard Nkundiye	Camp Kimihurura, Kigiali
Para-Commando Battalion	Commandant Aloys Ntabukuze	Camp Kanombe, Kigali
Huye Commando Battalion	Maj Alphonse Ntezilyayo	Kibungo
Ruhengeri Commando Battalion	Maj Augustin Bizimungu	Ruhengeri
Military Police Battalion	Commandant Emmanuel Neretse	Camp Kami, Kigali
Reconnaissance Battalion	Maj Ildephonse Rwendeye	Camp Kigali
Anti-Aircraft Battalion	Col Théoneste Bagosora	Camp Kanombe, Kigali
Air Squadron	Col Sébastien Ntahobali	Kigali IAP
Field Artillery Battery	Maj Aloys Mutabera	

Table 2: Equipment of the Air Squadron FAR, 1 October 1990

Aircraft	Registration	Notes
SE.210 Caravelle	9XR-CH	stored, waiting for buyer
Falcon 50	9XR-NN	VIP transport
SA.365C2 Dauphin	10K07 (c/n 5048)	VIP transport
BN-2A-9 Islander	9XR-GV	
BN-2A-21 Islander	9XR-GW	
Nord 2501 Noratlas	9XR-GX	stored, used as source of spares
Nord 2501 Noratlas	9XR-GY	
Rallye R.235 Guerrier	20L08	
AS.350 Ecureuil	10K14	
AS350 Ecureuil	10K15	
SA.342L Gazelle	10K09	rocket-armed
SA.342L Gazelle	10K10 (c/n 2004)	rocket-armed
SA.342L Gazelle	10K12 (c/n 2163)	cannon-armed

CHAPTER TWO:
RWANDAN PATRIOTIC ARMY

The movement that caused the ultimate demise of Juévnal Habyarimana's Second Rwandan Republic aroused from all the negative experiences different Rwandan communities went through – at home and abroad, but particularly in Uganda – during the 1960s and 1970s.

Uganda experienced nearly continuous political crisis and instability, civil wars, insurgencies and foreign invasions during its short history as an independent country. This background was to heavily influence the political and then military resurgence of the Tutsi refugees there – and do so long after the defeat of the UNAR.

That said, the presence of a significant Rwandan community in Uganda came into being due to different factors. In pre-colonial times, there were no fix borders but the area along which the borders were drawn since the early 1960s was a place where the influence of different kingdoms met. In the decades preceding the colonialization, Rwandan monarchs began extending their influence into this region – partially by establishing good ties with the Ankole Kingdom whose population was divided along similar lines in Rwanda (with the Hima being similar to Tutsi and the Hiru to the Hutu). Thus, when on 14 May 1910 the Anglo-German Treaty delimited precisely the boundaries between Ruanda and Uganda, thousands of ethnic Rwandans living in the Mufumbiro region (corresponding to what are nowadays Kabale and Kisoro Districts of Uganda) and loosely depending on Rwandan monarchs, found themselves under British rule and – later on – became Ugandan citizens.

Another wave of Rwandans – foremost Hutus – followed in the 1920s and 1950s, when forced labour and heavy taxation by Belgians caused many to emigrate. The events in Rwanda of 1959 and subsequent years of unrest caused two additional waves of – primarily Tutsi – refugees known, as mentioned above, as '59ers'. Of the 336,000 Rwandan refugees accounted for by the UN Refugees Agency (UNRA) by late 1964, 200,000 were in Burundi, 36,000 in Tanzania, 22,000 in Tanzania, and 78,000 in Uganda.

The first of refugees that reached Uganda in 1959-1964 period were classified by British authorities as 'illegal immigrants' and expelled: when the number of refugees trying to cross the border increased the British – for various reasons – denied them access to the country. Nevertheless, 7,562 Rwandans reached Uganda between May and September 1962 alone. Uganda's independence of 9 October 1962, changed the situation to some degree – foremost because the new authorities expected the Rwandans to stay for a short period of time. Instead, some of exiles settled with relatives already living in the country but others were sent to camps established in western Uganda. Because of an economic crisis; because the local Hutu saw the newly-arrived Tutsi as unwelcome economic competitors; but also because the Tutsi refugees from Rwanda were fast to start establishing ties with their Hima cousins in the Ankole region and thus became involved in the local struggle with the Hiru, Kampala changed its politics subsequently. Contrary to Tanzania – where President Julius Nyerere favoured an assimilation of Rwandan refugees, allowed them to disperse, to buy and own land, and granted them citizenship – most of the 59ers in Uganda remained herded in refugee camps, primarily located in remote areas. Living from small farming plots and international aid, they vegetated for years while growing a new generation of youngsters on memories of their homeland they could hardly hope to ever see again. Their future did not appear particularly bright because they were de-facto 'barely tolerated foreigners'.

Overall situation of Rwandan – and especially Tutsi – refugees in Uganda evolved in January 1971 when CoS Ugandan Army, Idi Amin, toppled the government of Milton Obote. Majority of Rwandan Tutsi in Uganda welcomed Amin's rule because of Obote's prosecution of members of Ankole ethnic group, early on. Their hopes for improvement of their position experienced the high point when Amin offered asylum to King Kiger V, then living in Tanzania. However, the refugee situation worsened dramatically because Amin began suspecting them of sympathising with Milton Obote's unsuccessful invasion attempt launched from Tanzania, in September 1972.

Indeed, the situation of Rwandans in Uganda became a sort of a paradox. On one hand, the government in Kampala regularly misused them as scapegoats for the worsening economic situation; on the other, Tutsi were recruited into the state-security apparatus – and particularly into the infamous State Research Bureau – because, deprived of any political basis in Uganda, they did not represent any kind of a threat for Amin. Finally, their involvement in repression of oppositionals had the effect of further alienating the refugee community in the eyes of the Ugandan population.

Nevertheless, the children of 59ers grew into a rapidly changing political landscape. The UNAR – whose cadres began to enjoy good life in Kampala – slowly lost its influence inside refugee camps. Some of Tutsi of poor origin found exile in the West, where they became relatively wealthy; while nobles that remained inside refugee camps fell into poverty. All of this resulted in the traditional order falling apart.

Furthermore, regardless of what origin, many children of the 59ers were highly educated. As usually in such cases, the reasons were rather ironic by nature: before 1986, Uganda retained some of harshest refugee laws in the region. Refugees were confined to designated camps and refugee status was transferred between generations: children born in Uganda from refugee parents were themselves considered refugees. However, the refugee status granted these children access to United Nations aid, including scholarships from the UN High Commissioner for Refugees (UNHCR) in particular.

Despite all of these issues and increasing separation, the entire community of Rwandan Tutsi in Diaspora continued maintaining strong ties. Although most of families had members living in entirely different countries, they maintained contact to each other, and not only Rwandan students living abroad were collecting money to pay for the scholarship of children in Uganda: they began establishing political and economic ties to the USA and Great Britain too. Gradually, new political organisations began to develop. At first, these movements were classic cultural associations, organising traditional activities; before soon they began generating ever more-intense political debates sustained by publications like Impuruza magazine in California (USA), or Muhabura in Burundi.

Troops and one of the Type-62 light tanks of the 208 Brigade JWTZ seen during the advance on Jinja – the second largest city in Uganda – on 18 April 1979. (Albert Grandolini Collection)

Thus came into being an entirely new generation of Rwandan refugees in Uganda – one that was eventually to succeed where the Inyenzi had failed. Its opportunity offered itself when Uganda entered another cycle of violent political crisis and war.[26]

Ugandan Liberation War

The bizarre, brutal and oppressive rule of Idi Amin caused thousands of political opponents to flee abroad. Many of them – including former president Milton Obote – found a safe haven in Tanzania. They were welcomed by the President Julius Nyerere who even agreed to back an attempt to topple the government in Kampala. On 15 September 1972 Obote's followers invaded Uganda in a three-prong operation that included attempted deployment of a commando force to Entebbe IAP, south of Kampala, on board a hijacked Kenyan Douglas DC-9 airliner. This part of the operation was spoiled when due to a pilot mistake on landing at Kilimanjaro airfield, and about 100 waiting commandos were never delivered to their destination. Meanwhile, two other groups – totalling about 1,670 combatants – launched a ground attack over the Tanzanian border in direction of the town of Mbarara. On 17 September 1972, both groups were crushed in vicious counter-attack by Ugandan Army units, and scattered: only 887 out of 1,340 involved fighters from the big group were ever accounted again. The smaller group of 330 was nearly annihilated: only 46 survivors came back to Tanzania. During the following weeks, Fouga CM.170 Magister and Mikoyan i Gurevich MiG-17s fighter bombers of the Ugandan Army Air Force (UAAF) flew a series of strikes on border villages in Tanzania and suffered extensive losses. Foremost, the assumption that this invasion would be sufficient to ignite a widespread popular uprising proved tragically wrong: some unrest and riots in Jinja and Kampala were quickly crushed by the military that remained loyal to Amin.

This incident marked the beginning of years of high tensions between Uganda and Tanzania, as not only Obote's followers began to gather there again, but new opposition movements came into being too. One of the latter was the Front for National Salvation

Tanzanian troops inspecting the wreckage of UAAF MiG-21s at Entebbe, in mid-April 1979, after overrunning this critically important installation. A few days later they were in control of Kampala too. (Pit Weinert Collection)

(FRONASA), established by Yoweri Museveni after his studies at the University of Dar es-Salaam. Over the time, Museveni established ties with representatives of the *Frente de Libertação de Moçambique* (Mozambiquan Liberation Front, FRELIMO) that was fighting against Portuguese rule in the latter country. During the mid-1970s, the FRONASA developed a small core of about 30 men trained by the FRELIMO. Starting in 1977-1978 period, Museveni also began receiving support from President Nyerere, who saw this organisation as an important player in the galaxy of exiled Ugandan politicians, and a good counter-weight to Obote's party.

Following a significant military build-up in Uganda and Tanzania with help of armament from the PRC and the USSR, tensions between the two countries increased through 1978. Amin's rule was not only ruining the Ugandan economy: after surviving several assassination attempts he turned increasingly mistrustful of even his closest aides and followers, and frequently reshuffled top military commanders. When this began causing dissent, fake intelligence reports were released about Tanzania concentrating troops on the mutual border

Yoweri Kaguta Museveni, leader of the NRA, as seen in the mid-1980s. His interpretation of Mao Zedong's theories of the revolutionary war and leadership of the insurgency in Uganda were to provide critical impulses for the development of the RPA. (UPDF)

A youthful Fred Rwigyema with a group of Western journalists in the 1980s. Rwigyema was one of the first 27 insurgents under Museveni's command. (UPDF)

with intention of invading Uganda. In turn, on 22 October 1978, one of Amin's favourite generals ordered the two elite units of the military into an invasion of Kagera Salient, in north-western Tanzania. Taken by surprise, the sole battalion of the Tanzanian military deployed in the area rapidly withdrew south of the Kagera River, while the Ugandans began terrorizing the local population, murdering, raping and looting in big style.

After mobilizing and significantly expanding its ground forces and its air wing, the Tanzanian military counter-attacked in mid-November and forced the Ugandans into a quick withdrawal north of the border. In agreement with his top military commanders and Ugandan exiles, Nyerere then decided to launch a counter-invasion and capture the towns of Mutukula, Mbarara and Masaka, in southern Uganda. Once there, he intended to let Obote's and Museveni's men continue the advance on Kampala and topple Amin.

After softening enemy positions in front of Mutukula with nearly one month artillery barrage, the Tanzanians assaulted and captured Mutukula in late January 1979. The operations against Mbarara and Masaka began soon after with steady advance of five Tanzanian brigades, reinforced by contingents of Ugandan insurgents and well-supported by mortars, artillery and Soviet-made BM-21 multiple rocket launchers (MRLS). Masaka was captured relatively easily, in March 1979, following a fierce artillery barrage that scattered Ugandan units deployed in the area. Ugandan Army offered slightly more serious resistance in Mbarara area, but was eventually defeated there too.

Although the Tanzanian invasion proved highly popular between the population of southern Uganda, contrary to Obote's expectations, the capture of border towns did not prompt any kind of a popular uprising against Amin. Therefore, Nyerere was forced to order his troops to continue in direction of Kampala.

Meanwhile, Libya launched a military intervention in support of Amin and Lockheed C-130 Hercules transports of the Libyan Arab Air Force began deploying a company of T-54 tanks, several batteries of artillery and BM-21 MRLSs from the Libyan Arab Army, and 2,500 members of the Libyan Popular Militia equipped with Land Rovers mounting 106mm recoilless rifles to Entebbe. While this

deployment was known to Tanzanians, they did not learn about Amin's order for Libyans – reinforced by last mechanised units of his army – to launch a swift advance and re-take Masaka. So it happened that the mixed Libyan-Ugandan force frontally collided with one of Tanzanian brigades, starting the battle of Lukaya.

Lukaya is a small town at the southern end of a 20km (13 miles) long causeway connecting Kampala with southern Uganda. The Libyan-Ugandan attack took the Tanzanians by surprise and scattered their central brigade, which primarily consisted of militiamen. However, Tanzanian commanders then de-toured one of their elite brigades and hit the enemy in the flank and the back. The battle of Lukaya ended with a disaster for Libyans and Ugandas, as their forces suffered a combined loss of more than 400 killed in exchange for few injured Tanzanians. It was a decisive encounter of this war too, then afterwards Libyans began to flee while Amin's troops ceased offering serious resistance.

In late April 1979, Tanzanian units thus approached Kampala and secured Entebbe. As next, they moved on Ugandan capital and encircled it, but left one venue of escape open for Libyans in order to save them from complete humiliation. Unknown to them, the same route was then used by Amin to flee into exile in Libya too. By early May 1979, Tanzanians secured Jinja and Tororo, and then continued with Gulu until reaching the Sudanese border near Lira, where the last serious clash of this war took place.[27]

Failed Transition

While the Tanzanian counter-invasion and occupation of Uganda thus ended eight years of terror spread by Amin's rule, it brought no peace. On the contrary: although representatives of all the Ugandan opposition movements agreed to unite under the aegis of the Uganda National Liberation Front (UNLF), and regroup their insurgent groups into the Uganda National Liberation Army (UNLA) during a conference in Moshi, in Tanzania, in March 1979, there was lots of disunity and rivalries. Headed by Yusufu Lule, the government they appointed and that was inaugurated on 13 April 1979 (two days after Tanzanians took Kampala) was dismissed already on 20 June of the same year, and Lule replaced by Godfrey Binaisa. Binaisa was in turn

Paul Kagame (first from right) joined the UNLA in 1979 and then the NRA in 1980. Ironically, after intelligence-related training on Cuba, he was sent for a course at the International Military and Educational facility of Fort Leavenworth, USA – where this photograph was taken in 1990. (Paul Kagame Collection)

Rwigyema with a group of Rwandan exiles that joined the NRA in the mid-1980s. (UPDF)

demoted in May 1980, and a provisional government titled 'Military Commission' – the 'shadow cabinet' that was actually running the country ever since Obote's fall – took over until the elections held in December the same year. Museveni received the post of the Minister of Defence in this government, but his work was hampered by activity of his two most important subordinates, Maj Gen Tito Okello and Brig David Oyite Ojok, both of whom were close associates of Milton Obote. All the FRONASA combatants that joined the UNLA were subjected to harsh treatment designed to weed them out: many were classified unfit for service or posted faraway from the capital, others forced to resign or sent for training to Tanzania. Disappointed, Museveni founded the Uganda Patriotic Movement (UPM) during the run for elections, but this had little chance against much more experienced, better-organised and Tanzanian-supported Uganda Conservative Party (UPC) led by Obote, and the old and well-established Democratic Party. While the UPC drew its support form the peripheral regions of Uganda, especially the North, the DP and the Conservative Party were popular in the centre of the country. Eventually, the UPC won the elections, obtaining 72 out of 126 seats in the Parliament, followed by the DP with 51 seats, and the Conservative Party. The UPM won only one seat.

Museveni contested results of the elections, denouncing them as heavily rigged, but Obote was appointed President of Uganda for second time and soon launched a wave of repression against the UPM, jailing many of its activists. The UPC's rule was heavily contested by other parties too, but while the Democratic Party opted for legal opposition, other groups chose to launch an armed struggle.

Former elites close to Amin established the Uganda National Rescue Front (UNRF) and the Former Uganda National Army (FUNA) in the North, while Yusufe Lule created the Uganda Freedom Fighters (UFF) in the centre, and this was soon followed by emergence of the Uganda Freedom Movement (UFM). Meanwhile, Museveni fled from Kampala and began gathering the cadre of former FRONASA-members to establish the Popular Resistance Army (PRA). Except for the UNRF, all of these groups were relatively small and poorly armed and equipped, but this was to some degree equalised by Tanzanian withdrawal from Uganda, in June 1981.

Early on, the UFM proved the strongest of insurgent movements, often launching spectacular operations. However, attracting primarily the middle class of the Baganda ethnic group, it also proved unable to widen its political basis and progressively declined after a failed assault on Kampala, on 22 February 1982. This not only triggered a bloody repression against its supporters in the capital, but also prompted the UNLA into a series of offensives that inflicted heavy casualties to the insurgents.

The UNRF and the FUNA remained confined to the north of Uganda, where they periodically held large swaths of the country under control. While in theory this left the PRA as the only adversary of the government in central Uganda, in reality it was so that the UNLA remained busy destroying the UNRF and the FUNA for long enough for Museveni's group to organise and arm.

Namely, the PRA was initially a rather small and very poorly equipped group attracting very little attention from the Ugandan public. It opened its armed struggle on 6 February 1981 with an unsuccessful attack on the armoury of Kabamba military base by 34 insurgents armed with 27 fire-arms. The situation began to change when Museveni met Yusuf Lule in Kenya, in June 1981 and the two decided to merge their organisations into the National Resistance Movement (NRM), with an armed branch titled the National Resistance Army (NRA). Cooperation with Lule was important for Museveni because the older politician represented majority of Baganda population in the strategic area known as Luweero Triangle, composed of five districts north of Kampala and traversed by three major roads. Namely, as a Hima from the Ankole group, Museveni had no sympathisers within majority of Ugandan population; however, with Lule's support, he suddenly became able to compete with the UFM and other insurgent movements in regards of attracting more widespread support, foremost within the Baganda ethnic group.

Bush War

The establishment of the NRM/NRA and preoccupation of Obote's government and the UNLA with obliteration of the UNRF and UFM bought plenty of time for Museveni. Foremost, it offered him an opportunity to prepare his movement for a protracted guerrilla

Rwigyema as Major-General and Deputy Commander of Museveni's National Resistance Army after the capture of Kampala in the period of January-February 1986. (NakedChiefs)

Colonel Alexis Kanyarengwe (left), formerly a close associate of Juvénal Habyarimana, was appointed the Vice President of the RPF in 1989. (RPF)

war along Mao Zedong's revolutionary warfare doctrine (although is ideology was always very different from that of the Chinese communists). The NRM/NRA was foremost a nationalist movement seeking to overcome ethnic identities as a pre-requisite to build a new, successful and modern Uganda, free from tragic divisions of the past. Contrary to other Ugandan insurgent movements of the time, Museveni's organisation went to great extension to establish close cooperation with local population. It build up a network of clandestine village-committees tasked with providing food and recruits, and organising political meetings. Over the time, the NRA began creating no-go zones for government troops and confining the UNLA inside urban areas, in turn bringing ever more population under its control. Also contrary to other insurgent groups – but foremost to the ill-disciplined Army – the NRA combatants were trained to follow a very strict code of conduct, primarily designed to preserve the goodwill of civilians. For example: rape was punishable by death sentence. All the NRA units had a Political Commissar responsible not only for political education and morale of its fighters, but also for continuous interaction with them, continuous interaction with locals, and continuous interaction between the population and the insurgents.

In comparison, inadequately trained, often poorly paid and poorly motivated UNLA soldiers were primarily recruited from northern Uganda and considered aliens by most of the population. They lacked discipline and tended to behave like an occupation force. As the conflict intensified, the government and its military began implementing brutal repression against the population of Luweero Triangle, considering it as collectively responsible for cooperation with Insurgents. Over the time, most of the area was depopulated: tragically, up 50% of the local population was murdered by the UNLA.[28] Unsurprisingly, even if it included an implicit coercive side, over the time the NRA's policy gained widespread support from the population of the Luweero Triangle.

By 1982, Museveni established several zonal forces – small units of about 200 men and 60 fire-arms each – as his main striking force. For their support, he encouraged creation of numerous semi-independent, local, part-time militias raised too. The most important of zonal forces – the Task Force led by Matayo Kyaligonza – began operating inside Kampala, where it targeted military bases and police stations, triggering another, often indiscriminate wave of repression

by government's security services. Although always impeded by a near-endemic lack of arms, ammunition and equipment, the NRA continued to expand and by the end of the same ear established its First Mobile Force, a four-company battalion capable of operating outside the Luweero Triangle too.

The NRA-build-up continued attracting ever more attention from the government and starting with Operation Bonanza, launched in June 1982, the UNLA run no less but 16 major campaigns against Museveni's group. Usual insurgent reaction – careful retreat while setting up ambushes along enemy lines of communication – proved highly effective and the NRA survived most of these without suffering heavy casualties. Serious crisis occurred only in period January-March 1983, when the largest government offensive forced the insurgents to abandon their bases inside Luweero Triangle and withdraw towards the north. This setback could have had very negative consequences wasn't it that on 2 December of the same year, the CoS UNLA, Major General (Maj Gen) David Oyite Ojok, was killed in a helicopter accident. The loss of this charismatic and popular leader can be seen as a sort of a death blow for Obote's presidency too. Not only that the president took months to find a suitable replacement, but the entire military never recovered form this loss and began suffering from internal rivalries and lack of cohesion caused by rifts between different ethnic groups.

The NRA exploited the opportunity to recover and expand the Mobile Force into a three-battalions-strong Mobile Brigade, in late 1983. One of first major operations of this unit was a surprise attack on the garrison of Matadi, launched on 20 February 1984 following a 110-kilometres (68.3 miles) long march. After a short fight, the insurgents captured 765 rifles and vast amount of ammunition. In another similar operation, the Mobile Brigade overrun the Kabamba garrison on 1 January 1985, capturing 650 rifles, five machine guns and 90,000 rounds of ammunition. Combined, these and other operations enabled a further expansion of the insurgency and in March 1985, Museveni dispatched his 11th Battalion into Western Uganda, thus opening the 'second front' in the war.

Few months later, the Mobile Brigade NRA fought a three-days-long battle against the UNLA's crack Special Brigade, an outfit

An RPF insurgent in the process of loading a mortar calibre 81 or 82mm. Like most of the fighters that joined the Front in 1990, he was wearing an ex-East German Army's summer uniform, easily recognisable by the rain-drop pattern in green on a stone grey background. (Adrien Fontanellaz Collection)

custom-tailored to eliminate insurgency. In the course of this clash, the military suffered a loss of between 200 and 300 casualties while inflicting only 24 losses to the NRA. While this clash could hardly have been described as a 'disaster' for the large Ugandan military, the psychological impact sent the shockwaves through all of its ranks. It widened the rift between various ethnic groups inside the UNLA too – foremost between the Langi that, belonging to the same ethnicity like the president, tended to be promoted more quickly, and the Acholi, often considered mere 'cannon fodder'. In June 1985, such differences resulted in a shoot-out inside the garrison of Jinja when Acholi soldiers refused to be sent to western Uganda to fight the NRA.

Talk and Fight

General lack of discipline and growing inter-ethnic tensions within Ugandan military eventually resulted in a coup d'état against President Obote. Led by Brigadier-General (Brig Gen) Bajilio Okello, this culminated with a three-days-long advance of one of UNLA units from northern Uganda on Kampala, which resulted in ousting of the government, on 27 July 1985. The new strongman, Tito Okello (not related to Bajilio) soon entered negotiations with different insurgent groups, and was successful in attracting the remnants of the UNRF

and various elements of the Former Uganda National Army (FUNA) to his side. Some of troops and units rallied in this fashion proved a valuable addition to the new government, foremost because they were much more disciplined than the UNLA – which was meanwhile in complete disarray. However, Okello's negotiations with the NRA were anything but easy and although beginning in August 1985, were not concluded before December of the same year.

Meanwhile, Museveni took advantage of complete disorganisation of the UNLA and sent different NRA units into a major offensive over most of Uganda. In the west, they captured towns like Fort Portal, Kasese and Mubende, while in the south they put the garrisons of Masaka and Mbarara under siege. Initially, the insurgents encountered fierce resistance, but by December 1985, most of defenders were on the brink of starvation and had to give up.

While the UNLA's resistance in Masaka and Mbarara de-facto immobilised most of the NRA for nearly two months, Okello proved unable to do anything to reinforce besieged garrisons. Museveni was thus left free to vastly expand his organisation. Thanks to an elaborate and sophisticated training system, he had more than 15,000 well-trained and motivated fighters under arms by January 1986, and was ready for his biggest coup: advance on Kampala. The Order of Battle of the NRA as of the time is provided in Table 3).

The final battle for Ugandan capital was over within only two days. Following advance of nearly all of NRA's mobile forces into positions around the city, Museveni's brother Salim Salleh launched an all-out attack supported by all available heavy weapons on 24 January 1986. Skilfully manoeuvring and exploiting the terrain, the insurgents overcame several UNLA positions that offered fierce resistance, killing around 80 and capturing more than 3,000 troops. Nevertheless, around 9,000 government troops escaped – together with their families – with help of an isolated counter-attack that prevented the NRA from sealing all exits from Kampala.[29]

Table 3: NRA Order of Battle, January 1986[30]

Unit	Commanding
Special Force	Jet Mwebaze
1st Battalion	Pecos Kutesa
3rd Battalion	Patrick Lumumba
5th Battalion	Steven Kashaka
7th Battalion	Matayo Kyaligonza
9th Battalion	Julius Chihandae
11th Battalion	Chefe Ali
13th Battalion	Yvan Koreta
15th Battalion	Samson Mande
19th Battalion	Peter Kerim
21st Battalion	Benon Tumukunde

Rwandan Refugees and the NRA

Two young friends that grew up in the community of Rwandan Tutsi refugees in Uganda were to play a decisive role in the genesis of the RPA. Originally, they decided to rally Museveni's movement because they believed that martial skills would be necessary to – sometime in the future – 'return' to Rwanda. Over the time, this decision was to prove necessary for protection of their community.

The first between them was Fred Rwigyema, who joined the FRONASA already in 1976, immediately after completing high school. Rwigyema was one of 29 men led by Museveni that were trained by FRELIMO in Mozambique, in December the same year. Following the fall of Idi Amin, he was not permitted to join the UNLA but was retained as bodyguard by Museveni. He participated in the failed attack on Kabamba barracks and later formed the nucleus around which the NRA was established. The former first Commanding Officer (CO) of the Mobile Force (back in 1982), Rwigyema obviously proved as skilled and dependable enough by Museveni to be assigned the command of the 11th Battalion when this was deployed to open the 'second front', in western Uganda.

The second was Paul Kagame, who joined the UNLA in early 1979 and was sent for a six-month training course as intelligence officer to Tanzania, in December of the same year, together with 60 other soldiers.[31] Kagame subsequently defected to the NRA and was involved in Kabamba attack; later on, he was attached to Chairman of NRA's High Command – Museveni himself. During the early 1980s, Kagame run a number of intelligence gathering missions against the UNLA, but was also responsible for preventing dissent among the movement and shielding its leadership from any internal threat. Thus, while Rwigyema grew into a renowned fighter and popular leader, Kagame gained reputation of a strict disciplinarian, and was more feared than loved among NRA's cadre.[32]

Through the early 1980s, Rwandan refugees in Uganda were repeatedly targeted by Obote's security services under the accusation of complicity with Museveni – but foremost because of regional political dynamics and competition for land and cattle in western Uganda. Indeed, creating much confusion for foreign observers, Kampala launched a propaganda campaign presenting Museveni as a Rwandan because of old cultural ties between his ethnic group, the Hima, and the Tutsi. This campaign reached a point where the UPC militia and security services launched a wave of repression against the refugees, causing tens of thousands of them to search for safety in refugee camps deeper inside Uganda, while their cattle was confiscated. A group of between 8,000 and 10,000 that attempted to flee back to Rwanda was denied access to their country and had to survive under very precarious conditions in the no-man's land between the two borders.

Such events and the presence of two young Tutsi among insurgents began attracting other volunteers from the community of Rwandan refugees, among them Chris Bunyenyezi and Peter Bayingana, who joined in 1984. Many more were to follow: by 1986, the NRA included a significant number of combatants of Rwandan origin.[33]

NRA School[34]

The capture of Kampala by the NRA did not end the Bush War. On the contrary: collapse of Obote's government, presence of many ex-UNLA troops, and often heavy-handed attitude of new government resulted in a number of insurgencies in northern Uganda. The emergence of these prompted Museveni to massively expand the NRA in order to become capable of countering this host of internal

threats. In July 1986, the Uganda People's Democratic Army emerged within the Acholi ethnic group, and began attacking governmental forces. Nearly simultaneously, prophetess Alice Lauma created her own para-military movement, the Holy Spirit Mobile Forces, and began assaulting the NRA but also other insurgent groups.

The resulting build-up of the NRA offered plenty of opportunities for Rwandan refugees to enlist and gain military experience, but also for veterans of the Bush War to reach higher positions within the hierarchy. Unsurprisingly, ever more of 'children of the 59ers' participated in the armed struggle that followed. In October 1987, they played important role in the destruction of the Holy Spirit Mobile Forces during its attempted advance on Kampala.[35] Following this defeat, Alice Lauma fled to Kenya and it took her successor – Joseph Kony – months to resurrect a new, similar movement. Meanwhile, lengthy negotiations and skilful political manoeuvring by Museveni culminated in the Peace Treaty with the UPDA, signed on 3 June 1988. Immediately afterwards, the insurgents of this group were integrated into the NRA.

Despite this influx of Northerners into Uganda military, Rwandans continued gaining ever more important positions – not only because of their own merits, but also through supporting each other in enhancing their careers. Initially, Museveni was keen to not only tolerate but also promote this process because he was certainly aware of Rwandan intention to 'return' to their homeland and thus saw them as no threat for his government. Indeed, before soon intentions of so many Rwandans that served with the NRA became a sort of public secret in Kampala. A person that used to live in the city at the time recalled:

'The Batutsi-Rwandans made a good part of the NRA. Many of insurgent officers were Rwandans, and hardly any of them could speak French... People of Kampala – most are Baganda – were a bit suspicious of these 'Westerners' at first, but then they brought peace and stability, so business could start again, and they liked it.... Later on we learned there was a deal between Rwandans and Museveni, and this was, 'we help the Banyankole (Museveni's tribe from western Uganda) to get rid of the Obote, Okelo and Acholi, then they help us get back to Kigali'. That's exactly what happened.'[36]

As soon as the NRM government gained international recognition, it began sending its military personnel abroad for further training. For example, Paul Kagame led a group of 67 cadets that received a nine-months training in intelligence in Cuba.[37] Meanwhile, Fred Rwigyema was assigned the overall command of the NRA's COIN campaign in northern Uganda.

When formal military ranks were introduced in the new Ugandan military, in January 1988, Rwigyema was promoted in rank to Major-General (Maj Gen) and assigned the post of the Chief-of-Staff and Vice-Minister for Defence. At the same time, Paul Kagame was promoted in rank to that of a Major and assigned the post of Deputy Director of the Directorate of Military Intelligence.[38]

During the following years, other Tutsi officers reached important positions within the NRA too. Majors Chris Bunyenyezi, Samk Kaka, and Peter Bayingana were in charge of the newly-established 306th Brigade, the Military Police and the Directorate of Medical Services, respectively. Captain Charles Musitu led the Directorate of Training and Recruitment – one of most important posts within the NRA – and even the Presidential Protection Unit included two Captains of Rwandan origin, while more than 90% of personnel in the IT services should have been Rwandan Tutsi.

Running Out of Time

The late 1980s were not only marked by the emergence of an entire generation of combat-proven Rwandan refugees, but also their political resurgence. Fundamental for the latter development was the establishment of the Rwandese Refugee Welfare Foundation (RRWF), already in 1979. Originally responsible for collecting and providing relief aid, the RRWF became politically-oriented and was renamed the Rwandese Alliance for National Unity (RANU), that began publishing its own newspaper ('The Alliancer') and promoting Rwandan identity as the mean to overcome the divide between Hutu and Tutsi. During its first few years of existence, majority of RRWF/RANU members were intellectuals with very different political backgrounds; some were nostalgic for the monarchist order, while others more sensitive for leftist ideas. Led by an executive committee, the RANU began organising an annual congress, the first of which took place in Uganda. From 1981, such meetings were held in Nairobi, in Kenya.

During the seventh RANU Congress, in December 1987, the movement adopted an eight-points programme, and re-named itself the Rwandan Patriotic Front (RPF) Inkotanyi. Subsequently, its members increased their efforts to gain additional support for the 59ers all over Africa and in the West and, in 1988, they began establishing a number of clandestine cells inside Rwanda – although with mixed results. Namely, while attempting to attract support from Rwandan Hutu too, the RPF failed to transmit their political views among the population. Eventually, the only value of such cells proved to be the intelligence they were capable of collecting.[39]

In 1989, Fred Rwigyema was elected the president of the RPF and, in September the following year, Col Alexis Kanyarengwe – formerly a close associate of Juvenal Habyarimana – was appointed the vice-president of the movement.[40]

The success of the NRA in combat against different Ugandan insurgencies and its triumph against the government of Milton Obote soon resulted in ever increasing pressure upon the RPF-leaders to repeat the exercise in Rwanda too. It was already in spring of 1986 that Museveni felt force to – following revelations about their numbers and influence in the Ugandan opposition press – arrest and lightly sanction a number of hot-headed Tutsi officers and other ranks for their plot to use the NRA for an invasion of Rwanda. Another incident occurred in early 1989, when 28 youngsters armed with 8 rifles had crossed the border to launch an insurrection on their own, and the RPF was forced to deploy a small party to find them and bring them back to Uganda. More importantly, it was the presence of numerous Rwandans in the NRA's hierarchy that became a source of discontent among other Ugandan ethnic groups, foremost the Baganda – whose support was essential for stability of Museveni's government. This became an urgent issue after it became known that Tutsi soldiers were particularly brutal against civilian population in

the course of various COIN operations in the north of the country. Justified or not, such reputation caused immense problems once the NRA began to integrate ex-UPDA combatants, although the later proved much less disciplined and certainly more likely to become involved in atrocities against civilians.[41]

The involvement of Rwandan Tutsi officers in the increasingly vicious COIN campaign waged by the NRA against various insurgent groups had also another – more sinister – effect upon them. Henceforth, persistent rumours circulated in the NRA about the willingness of the Rwandans (whether officers, NCOs or other ranks) to use excessive force – including large-scale executions – against civilians in order to dissuade them from support of insurgents. Considering it was a very convenient practice for Ugandan NRA-officers to misuse their Rwandan brothers-in-arms as scapegoats for most of large-scale violations of human rights, most of such accusations should be taken with a pinch of salt. However, at least one case of atrocities committed by NRA-unit under the command of a Rwandan Tutsi officer is well-documented: the Mukara massacre of July 1989, by the 106th Battalion NRA under the command of Chris Bunyenyezi.[42]

Additional motivation for Ugandan resentment of the Tutsi came from ever more arrogant and outright opportunistic behaviour of Rwandans settled in Uganda: as some quickly gained good jobs in NRM's administration, ever more of them expected similar treatment because of their high-placed siblings. Therefore, while 'his' Tutsi were a significant military asset, Museveni was forced to conclude that their presence and behaviour began causing discontent within his own political basis. Furthermore, while he easily ignored concerns expressed by Habyarimana's government in Kigali – which was well-aware of the RPF and its agenda, because Rwandan security services have managed to infiltrate this organisation – foreign supporters began exercising pressure upon Ugandan government to reduce the size of the Ugandan military, which by 1988 was gulping at least 3.87% of the Gross Domestic Product.[43] In need of foreign investment, Museveni was left without little choice but to start reducing the influence of Rwandan Tutsis within the NRA. For the Rwandan exiles this became obvious when CoS Maj Gen Elly Tumwine has left the service and was not replaced by his deputy, Fred Rwigyema.[44] Worse yet: in November 1989, Rwigyema was removed from his position.

Although the latter decision proved something like a blessing for the RPF (because the demotion of this popular and well-connected officer from the NRA enabled him to get elected as the president) it provided clear evidence that the best times of the Tutsi influence upon Museveni were over.

Indeed, during the following weeks and months, several other members of the Front were purged from their positions, and it became clear that Museveni would never stand to his promise to grant citizenship to the Rwandan exiles. With the RPF on the verge of losing its position in the military, concerns rose over its ability to launch an attack on Rwanda too: this convinced many of the Tutsi that they had no other choice left but to 'return to their homeland, right away'.[45]

Other Factors for the Start of War

Ugandan internal politics was not the only factor that prompted the RPF into military action. In February 1988, the Rwandan government agreed to the establishment of the Rwandan-Ugandan Joint Committee on the Refugee Question under the auspices of the UNHCR. This body was tasked with finding answers to the decades-old issue of refugees. During the Franco-African Summit of La Baule, in 1990, French President Francois Mitterand announced that France is going to favour all the countries willing to democratise. This call received a positive reply from Juvénal Habyarimana, who declared his intention to end the single-party rule in Rwanda.

While the leadership of the RPF and many observers saw these developments as mere political manoeuvring by Rwandan government, there was a real risk of Habyarimana's actions creating a rift within the community of exiled Tutsi and make it considerably harder for the Front to justify an attack on a 'young democracy' in Kigali. Furthermore, while the Front abysmally failed to penetrate the political scene inside Rwanda and thus remained fundamentally foreign to its supposed homeland, the few Hutu defectors that rallied the RPF tended to describe the government of Rwanda as weakened by the deep division between Northerners and Southerners, prone to fall if receiving even a moderate blow. Thus, as of 1990, Rwigyema and his aides had many reasons to act quickly and very few to further delay their old dreams of returning to their homeland.

Although pressed by the circumstances, the RPF had a number of favourable factors on its side. Its ideology – embedded in its eight-points program – was designed to attract as many supporters as possible (at least in Diaspora), without generating undue antagonism. Although a significant part of the Front's leadership could be grossly described as 'leftists', they also developed a political discourse rooted in the history and traditions of Rwanda.[46] Correspondingly, the RPF began using history to demonstrate that the events of 1959 were a deviation of the traditional society and using 'cultural troops' – like dancers – to rally support with exiled community.[47]

Nevertheless, the most important factor enabling the RPF to launch an invasion of Rwanda was the fact that it could rely on a group of highly experienced officers and NCOs for creation of its military wing – the Rwandan Patriotic Army (RPA). The existence of the men in question was invaluable because while new fighters could be trained in a matter of months, experienced and combat-proven leaders take years and lessons paid for in blood to form. Indeed, men like Rwigyema, Kagame, Bunyenyezi, Kaka, Bayingana, and others were in unique position of being insurgents that applied guerrilla tactics and then acting as officers of a regular military that fought conventional battles towards the end of the Bush War in Uganda, before being engaged in another COIN war again. Their institutional memory was very fresh and extremely rich on knowledge about the ways to wage mobile warfare while operating with an absolute minimum of resources in men and material.

Finally, the RPF had another important advantage: it could still rely for support and provision of bases on nearly symbiotic relationship with the leaders of the NRA hierarchy, who proved more than eager to support its struggle. Namely, it must be kept in mind that characters like Museveni and Rwigyema knew each other intimately since nearly two decades, and that the latter and Salim Saleh – Museveni's brother and former commander of the NRA – were close friends.[48] On the top of this, it is possible that the Rwandan Tutsi were aware about Museveni's World-view widely circulated within military circles in Great Britain: although this was little known at the time, he supported the idea of the ultimate formation of a confederation centred in Africa's central Rift Valley under hegemonic control by Hima and Tutsi rulers in Uganda, Rwanda, and Burundi.[49]

CHAPTER THREE:
INVASION

The decision that eventually triggered the Rwandan Civil War of 1990-1994 was taken during a telephone-conversation between Fred Rwigyema and Paul Kagame on 28 September 1990. Rwigyema was in Brussels while Kagame was undergoing course at the International Military and Educational Training facility of Fort Leavenworth, Kansas.[50] What exactly they intended to do and how did they expect to topple Habyarimana's government remains unclear and a matter of some controversy until today. Because all of involved officers had to hide their affiliation with the RPF, very few were involved in the planning of invasion, although the refugees' resolve to return to Rwanda was common knowledge since years. Certain is only that early October 1990 offered the RPF leadership a very good opportunity to launch its operation because Museveni and Habyarimana were to attend the UN World Summit for Children in New York. 9 October was also Uganda's independence day, which was always a good opportunity to move troops around the country. It is known that preparations for the invasion began as long as three months earlier, when RPF-members still serving with the NRA not only received an order to be on stand-by, but also undertook some limited logistical preparations. For example, hundreds of cattle were slaughtered to prepare dry meat rations.[51] Furthermore, the RPF obtained large stocks of summer uniforms of the former East German Army, and was able to issue these to its fighters right at the start of insurgency.

The most common perception is that Rwigyema and Kagame intended to advance on Kigali as fast as possible, exploit the moment of surprise and remove the government before the FAR could even mobilise. Considering Rwigyema's experience with the NRA's gradual growth in the course of a protracted guerrilla struggle this might appear unlikely, however.

Gathering the RPA

After having received one or two days' notice and being instructed to take with them as many weapons and ammunition as possible, the Rwandan soldiers began to desert from NRA units on 29 September 1990. Early the following morning, hundreds of men rallied a few kilometres from the border and were hastily formed in two battalions before entering Rwanda by assaulting the Kagitumba Border Post. The latter was defended by an isolated FAR platoon of the Mutara Independent Company, which was overwhelmed within few minutes. Actually, the garrison was taken by surprise and fled as soon as its commander – Warrant Officer (WO) Gasore – was killed and became the first casualty of the war. As next, the RPF captured the nearby Nyabwishongwezi, where their advance elements were reinforced by around 400 men mounted on trucks and led by Rwigyema, later in the afternoon.[52]

The convoy in question had left Kampala late in the evening the previous day and travelled the entire night before refuelling in Mbarara in mid-morning. This late departure from Kampala could have been caused by Rwigyema who, in order to avoid suspicion, reportedly assisted to a football match before taking the lead of the column.[53]

Meanwhile, there was a steady flow of deserters and by 2 October Rwigyema had four battalions with a total of between 2,000 and 2,500 men – including 3 majors, 15 captains, 100 lieutenants and NCOs – under his command when he announced them the foundation of the Rwandan Patriotic Army (for a full composition of the RPA in early October 1990, see Table 4). Most of the troops brought with them their fire-arms, but some managed to take with them heavier weapons too, including few mortars, several ZPU-4 quarduple machine guns, and two Type-63 multiple rocket launchers (MRL) calibre 107mm. Defectors from the Presidential Protection Unit NRA arrived in two vehicles equipped with advanced communication gear.[54]

Table 4: First Units of the RPA, October 1990

Unit	Commanding
1st Battalion	Chris Bunyenyezi
4th Battalion	Steven Ndugute
6th Battalion	Adam Waswa
9th Battalion	Sam Kaka

Crucial Context

Despite this apparently spontaneous and disorganised mobilisation, the RPF indeed managed to take both Museveni and Habyarimana by surprise. At first glance, this feat might appear almost miraculous as the refugees' project to take arms and return in Rwanda was an open secret: NRA fighters of Rwandan origin never made any kind of secret about their ultimate goal. Their operation was especially no surprise for Kigali either, because Rwandan military intelligence services have successfully infiltrated the RPF. However, although nearly everybody that mattered knew that something was in the air since months (if

The core of the RPF as seen at the start of insurgency, in late 1990 or early 1991. Notable are their uniforms of (East) German origin, large stocks of which were available on the international market in the early 1990s as result of German reunification and the end of the Cold War. (via Adrien Fontanellaz)

RPA insurgents seen entering Rwanda on board a Ugandan Army truck in early October 1990. While precious as a means of transportation, these vehicles proved a mixed blessing: most of them were destroyed by FAR Gazelles in a matter of days. (AF)

Another photograph of RPA insurgents in one of the few vehicles they took with them from the Ugandan military. Although battle-hardened, NRA veterans had never before engaged an enemy that could call for air support and thus were unprepared to encounter the aggressively deployed attack helicopters of the Rwandan military. (RPF)

not years) in advance, very few could knew when and how it would happen, especially as the largely ineffective and amateurish attempts of 1986 and 1989 further truncated the cards while, by strictly limiting the number of men involved in the pre-invasion planning process, the RPF leadership successfully maintained operational confidentiality until the last moment. Therefore, while the Ugandan President knew for sure about the general agenda of the RPF and was using it to pressure the Kigali regime to make concessions in order to find a peaceful solution to the

Fred Rwigyema, the highly popular first commander of the RPA, was killed in a controversial incident on 2 October 1990. (UPDF)

Paul Kagame after taking over the command of the RPA. (Adrien Fontanellaz Collection)

Maj Ildephonse Rwendeye, CO of the Reconnaissance Battalion and then the commander of the FAR Sector No.1 (or 'Gabiro Axis Task Force FAR'), skilfully led his troops in early battles against insurgents. He was killed in an ambush on 18 November 1990. (Adrien Fontanellaz Collection)

old problem of Rwandan refugees, it is very likely that he was genuinely surprised by the date of their invasion.[55]

Indeed, the ease at which the deserters managed to move around the country and to assemble near the Rwandan border does not necessarily imply that the NRA top leadership directly supported this action. Top NRA officers of Rwandan origin – foremost Maj Gen Fred Rwigyema and Lt Col Adam Waswa – were in a perfect position to prepare the invasion on their own – even more so when using the coming celebrations for Ugandan Independence Day as pretext. Another 'good excuse' was the fact that the NRA's administration was not effective enough to monitor all of its operations all the time, while it was 'normal' to move significant military contingents around the country because of various COIN operations. Of similar importance is the fact that Ugandan officers in the NRA did not attempt to interfere with the mass desertion of their Rwandan colleagues – either because they sympathised with their case or because they were happy to see them leave.[56]

Whatever was the case and despite embarrassing the President of Uganda (and, more importantly, the President of the OAU), Rwandans did not have to expect a harsh reaction from Museveni either, for reasons mentioned above. Events of the following years were to prove them right, then Ugandan authorities never stopped supporting them through sales of arms, ammunition and other supplies, permissions to use bases inside Uganda for training and refitting, and even through provision of diplomatic support (which in turn meant that from the very inception the RPA benefited from an invaluable asset for any insurgent group in its position: safe rear bases). Indeed, while roadblocks were established during the days after defection and invasion – primarily with the aim of preventing additional NRA-deserters from defections to the RPA – these were dismantled already by 6 October, and anybody arrested left free to continue his voyage in direction or Rwanda.[57]

Fog of War

Although taken by surprise, the FAR reacted quite quickly. In the absence of President Habyarimana, the FAR HQ in Kigali was led by Laurent Serubuga who acted promptly. In reaction to reports about attack on the border, he put the Reconnaissance Battalion, the Para-Commando Battalion, and the Engineering Company on alert, and then began ordering their elements - reinforced by the Byumba Independent Compnay – in direction of invaded zone. Therefore, it was already during the afternoon of 1 October that units dispersed along the border were put on alert and then under the command of the Commanding Officer (CO) of the Reconnaissance Battalion, Maj Ildephonse Rwendeye. However, early the following morning, an advance party composed of the Mutara Independence Company and a squadron of armoured cars from the Reconnaissance Battalion, supported by a platoon of 120mm mortars, was ambushed by the RPA while entering Matimba and forced to withdraw after a loss of four vehicles captured by enemy. This skirmish did not delay the RPA which meanwhile continued its advance along two parallel axes: one along the asphalted road to Gabiro and the second along a track leading to Nygatare and Ngarama. By 4 October 1990, elements of the 9th Battalion RPA captured Nyagatara while other units continued in direction of Gabiro.[58]

The arrival of reinforcements from Kigali enabled the FAR units in Ngarama area to finally stop the advance of the 9th Battalion RPA, and even start launching counter-attacks supported by mortar fire, during 5 October. Similarly, further east, other elements of the RPA were prevented from taking Gabiro by fierce resistance of the Para-Commando battalion – and despite several infiltration attempts.[59]

Two separate – and still highly controversial – incidents that took place during these first days of the war, were to have lasting influence upon the subsequent flow of the conflict. Late in the afternoon of 4 October 1990, several FAR units – including the crack Para-Commando Battalion – received the order to return to Kigali. Reasons for this remain unclear and are usually explained with lack of ammunition or even a supposed warning about an imminent RPA attack on the capital, allegedly provided by the US Embassy. Either way, this re-deployment significantly weakened the defences of Gabiro: the local garrison withdrew the following night and the town was captured by the 4th Battalion RPF without any resistance, on the morning of 5 October.[60]

Indeed, during that night citizens of Kigali were awakened a few minutes after 01.00hrs in the morning by the sound of intense fire from automatic weapons, and there are multiple reports about FAR units opening fire on unspecified targets.[61] While most of foreign observers latter described this incident as a deliberate show organised by the Rwandan government in order to dramatise the conflict and press its foreign allies into provision of additional military support, cases of overreaction by the FAR – perhaps even triggered by minor diversionary attacks by infiltrated elements of the RPA – cannot be excluded. Either way, the fashion in which Rwandan authorities reacted during the following days guaranteed that the government lost any chance of gaining support of the international media – because thousands of people, primarily Tutsi, were subsequently accused of sympathising with the RPF and arrested. Although most of prisoners were eventually released, hundreds were detained and herded at the Nyamirabo Stadium, where some were tortured and even 'disappeared'.[62] This highly visible and massive repression was nothing short of a strategic mistake for a government very much dependant on support of foreign powers, the authorities of which were highly sensitive to own public opinion. For example, the Belgian government, which accelerated delivery and paid for a shipment of small arms ammunition delivered to Kigali per Lockheed C-130 Hercules transports of the Belgian Air Force on 5 October 1990, suspended all further aid after fierce debate in its Parliament.[63]

Death of Commander Fred

Another, perhaps even more important event that marked the start of the war and remains extremely controversial until today took place on 2 October 1990 at Nyabwishongwezi, when the RPA lost its first commander, Fred Rwigyema.

Until today, multiple versions about what happened to him have appeared in the public, the most usually cited one being that he was killed by his men; more precisely, it should have been Maj Chris Banyingana that had shot him during a dispute about the strategy of RPA operations. Accordingly, Rwigyema insisted on a protracted guerrilla war while Banyingana advocated a swift advance straight for Kigali.[64]

Another version of the same event cites Lt Kato – a man recommended to Rwigyema by Kagame - to have been the murderer.[65] RPA's official version described this affair in a far more prosaic – though quite realistic – light. Accordingly, the commander was killed moments after having climbed to a hill to observe the development of a battle between his troops and

A still from a video showing FAR troops in the Mutara area, near the Kagitumba Border Post, in October 1990. (Adrien Fontanellaz Collection)

A VBL armoured car of the Reconnaissance Battalion FAR as seen in the Kagitumba area in late October 1990. (Adrien Fontanellaz Collection)

One of the Rwandan AML-90s as seen on the streets of Kigali in October 1990. (Albert Grandolini Collection)

a platoon of FAR armoured vehicles. Supposedly, a crew of the later was on retreat when it spotted a group of officers on top of a hill and briefly stopped to open fire on a fleeting target with a machine-gun. One bullet hit Rwigyema in the head, instantly killing him.[66]

Whatever was the actual reason of Rwigyema's death, this de-facto 'de-capitation' of the RPA on only the second day of invasion came at the worst possible moment and was clearly endangering the entire enterprise. Namely, the four hastily created RPA battalions were composed of men who – despite their extensive

Belgian officers with the pilot of one of SABENA's DC-10s used to transport them to Rwanda. (Albert Grandolini Collection)

The sole Rally Guerrier light strike aircraft of the FAR seen against the backdrop of Belgian paratroopers and a C-130 Hercules transport at Kayibanda IAP. Rwanda received two such aircraft (one in 1983 and another in 1984), valued at FF12 million but provided free of charge, but one crashed shortly after delivery. (Albert Grandolini Collection)

Belgian Para-Commandos mounted in an Iltis Jeep armed with two MAG general-purpose machine guns, on the streets of Kigali, in October 1990. (Albert Grandolini Collection)

experience in the NRA – were unaccustomed to operate together and had to learn to do so under trying circumstances, while conducting fast-paced offensive operations. As a result, numerous tactical mistakes were made – like units neglecting to occupy the high ground above their line of advance and thus exposing themselves to enemy counter-attacks. Worse yet, soon after the start of invasion, hundreds of untrained civilians began rallying the RPA from Uganda, adding further confusion and indiscipline. For example, they looted a beer depot in Nyagatare and remained there – drunk – for days, while after the fall of Gabiro, soldiers of the 4th Battalion looted that city's Guest House. Unsurprisingly, while Maj Peter Bayingana was assigned the duty of Temporary CO RPA, with Maj Chris Bunyenyezi as Deputy, the leadership of the Front decided to hide the news of Rwigyema's death for a while longer, in order to protect the morale of their fighters. However, in turn this later caused significant suspicion among the rank and file, and also prompted several commanders to order uncoordinated moves with their units, at their own discretion.[67]

Finally, there are opinions that since Rwigyema's death the RPA and the RPF began to follow a much more extremist and hard-line policy.

Foreign Intervention

As the battle was developing in north-eastern Rwanda, President Habyarimana was quick to request help from allies in Belgium, France and Zaïre. He called Jean-Christophe Mitterrand in Paris – head of the African Cell (an organ reporting directly to the Presidential office), and son of the French President François Mitterrand – to ask for support. Day later, he made a stop in Bruxelles and met the Belgian King Baudoin and Prime Minister Wilfried Martens.[68]

While Belgian government declined Rwandan request for help, and subsequently cancelled all deliveries of aid, the government in Brussels decided to deploy troops to protect the Belgian community of 1,630 civilians in the country, and evacuate it if necessary. For this purpose, it prepared a 535-strong detachment of the 2e Battalion Para-Commando (three companies) and one company of the *3e Battalion Parachutiste*, supported by a reconnaissance platoon, a mortar platoon, communications and medical units. The units in question were airlifted to Kigali IAP on board a Boeing 727 and C-130 transports of the Belgian Air Force, and Douglas DC-10 airliners of the SABENA within the frame of the Operation Green Bean, between 4 and 6 October 1990.

For a host of reasons, Paris proved particularly responsive to

A soldier from one of the Commando Battalion's FAR (note his red sash) guarding Kayibanda IAP, outside Kigali, in October 1990. (Albert Grandolini Collection)

A Zairian soldier seen together with a Rwandan VBL armoured car, at Kayibanda IAP, in October 1990. (Albert Grandolini Collection)

FAR troops and a Land Rover at one of the road-blocks outside Kigali, in October 1990. (Albert Grandolini Collection)

Habyarimana's call. Always keen to maintain its position in Africa the French government ignored the fact that it never provided any security guarantees against external threats to Rwanda. Furthermore, the French saw Belgium as a spent power, unable to do more but renounce its heritage of former colonial overlord of Zaïre, Rwanda and Burundi. Because of RPF's Ugandan origin and the fact that nearly all of insurgent leadership was English-speaking, Paris saw the insurgents as Ugandan proxies and their operation as a frontal attack against the Pré-carré – the French zone of influence in Africa: it could not let Habyarimana's government be overthrown by the RPA without reacting. Correspondingly, while not flying any air strikes requested by Rwandan President, nor letting its troops becoming directly involved against the RPA, Paris became heavily involved in providing support for the government in Kigali.[69]

During the night from 3 to 4 October 1990, the 4th Company

of the 2e *Régiment Étranger de Parachutistes* (2nd Foreign Parachutist Regiment, REP) and a communications detachment (total of 140 troops) embarked two C.160 Transall transport aircraft of the *Armée de l'Air* (French Air Force, AdA) that flew them from Bangui in the Central African Republic, to Kigali. On 5 October, they were reinforced by the 3rd Company of the 3e Régiment de Parachutistes d'Infanterie de Marine (3rd Marine Infantry Parachute Regiment, RPIMa) that arrived from Chad.[70]

While Belgian para-commandos secured the Gregoire Kayibanda IAP and the 12 kilometres long road connecting it to the capital, the French troops evacuated 313 French citizens. Two days later, Belgians deployed detachments to Ruhengeri (where the French troops rescued 165 foreigners), Gisenyi and Byumba to collect other expatriates.[71]

Meanwhile, Belgian government found itself confronted by fierce critique and was forced to order a withdrawal of its troops, on 27 October. Correspondingly, the last Belgian troops left Rwanda already on 1 November, and Operation Green Bean was officially declared for concluded.[72] Similarly, having completed its task, the 4th Company 2nd REP was repatriated on 20 October.

Despite this withdrawal, other contingents remained in country: at least 20 Belgian advisors continued serving in the Bigogwe Commando Training Centre, the FAR medical services and the Rwandan Army HQ until 1994.[73] Similarly, the other French military units remained in the country, now within the frame of Operation Noroît (Northern Wind). Finally, Col Gilbert Canovas of the French Army was officially assigned to the FAR HQ starting with 11 October 1990.[74]

Overall, although they never fought the RPA, the fact that Belgian and French troops secured several strategic installations in and around Kigali, enabled the FAR to deploy additional troops against insurgents. They left it to the third major ally of Rwanda – Zaïre – to provide more significant help. Commercial airliners brought 1,200 troops of the *Forces Armées Zairoises* (Zairian Armed Forces, FAZ) to Goma, from where they marched to Kigali between 5 and 10 October 1990. Led by Gen Mahele Lieko Bokungu this detachment included some of best FAZ units, including company of special forces troops of the *Service d'Action et de Renseignement Militaire* (Zairian Military Intelligence Service, SARM), one commando battalion of the *Division Spéciale Présidentielle* (Special Presidential Division, DSP), and the 313th Parachute Battalion of the (French-trained) 31st Parachute Brigade.[75]

Stalemate

Reinforced by units from Kigali, and with Belgian, French and FAZ contingents de-facto securing Kigali, the FAR was quick in preparing and launching a counter-offensive. The units in Mutara region were distributed into two sectors: one in the east and another in the west. Both sectors were provided ample air support by the Air Squadron FAR. When the war began, this unit had eight aircraft and helicopters in operational condition, including one Islander, one Guerrier, the Noratlas transport, two Ecureuils and three Gazelles. During the first 26 hours of the campaign it flew only reconnaissance sorties, but was then authorised to make

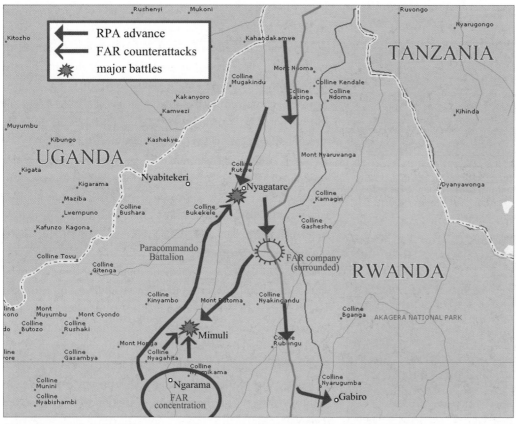

A map showing the initial RPA advance into north-eastern Rwanda in early October 1990.

The quarters of French paratroopers inside one of hangars at Kayibanda IAP in October 1990. Visible in the background is one of the FAR's Gazelle helicopters – obviously unserviceable and stripped down of all useful spares. (Albert Grandolini Collection)

use of its weapons. Then the flying became especially intensive: one armed with a 20mm cannon and the other two with unguided rockets, Gazelles flew as many as six attack sorties a day between 2 and 23 October 1990, spending a total of 640 rockets. Their pilots proved highly efficient and well-motivated – and they operated over an area they knew well, because Mutara region was often a scene of exercises in the months before the war. Unsurprisingly they achived notable success.

On 3 October 1990, a pair of Gazelles attacked and destroyed a truck convoy near Nutoma, while on 7 October they began supporting attacks on Gabiroa and Nyatagare. On the same day, the Air Squadron suffered its first casualties of the war, when the BN-2 flown by Maj Ruterena and Lt Hayugimana, was shot down by RPA's ground fire, and the crew killed. The unexpected presence of anti-aircraft machine guns in insurgent arsenal compelled other crews to subsequently operate either from higher altitudes during reconnaissance operations, or from very low altitudes dur-

ing attack operations.

The following day, on 8 October 1990, Maj Gen Mahele – assigned the overall command of the Western Sector – led the DSP-unit and the 313th Parachute Battalion FAZ, supported by one battalion of FAR infantry, into a counter-attack against Gabiro. After a day-long and intensive fighting, the RPA was forced to withdraw.[76] However, the reinforced 4th Battalion RPA counter-attacked and retook Gabiro already the following day, and began to pursue withdrawing Rwandans and Zairians down the paved road. In turn, the advance party of insurgents was ambushed by the FAR troops shortly before reaching Nyakayaga, and forced to retreat back to Gabiro.[77]

Supported by five AML-60 and AML-90 armoured cars of the Reconnaissance Battalion FAR, the combined Rwandan-Zairian force – whose troops began to war red bands around their arms to avoid friendly fire incidents – counter-attacked Gabiro on 10 and 13 October, and successfully entered it. However, the FAZ soldiers subsequently became more interested in looting the local Guest House: a fierce counter-attack of the RPA took them by surprise and forced them to withdraw after a loss of one AML-60 and one AML-90.[78]

Alarmed by reports about misbehaviour, indiscipline, harassment of civilians and looting, the Rwandan government then requested Kinshasa to recall the FAZ detachment and this was quickly repatriated to Goma. That said, while their deficiencies were real beyond any doubt, the Zairians also had a reason to complain as they were at least once hit by Gazelles, and several times came under fire by FAR ground units too. Furthermore, during their one week-long presence, they suffered a casualty rate of up to 10% while repeatedly denied ammunition resupply by their Rwandan allies.

Following FAZ withdrawal, Maj Ildephonse Rwendeye took over the command of the Sector No. 1 and filled the hole left by Zairians with the Huye Commando Battalion, the Gitarama Independent Company, and a newly-etablished battalion consisting of hastily-trained reservists or troops from non-combat services, 'corseted' by instructors from the Bigogwe Commando Training Centre.[79] The frontlines in Gabiro area subsequently steadied, and during mid-October the FAR considered the situation secure enough to replace the Huye Battalion with the Ruhengeri Commando Battalion (minus one company), another hastily assembled battalion of reservists, one company of Military Police, and a squadron from the Reconnaissance Battalion.[80]

While the Sector No. 2 – including the Ngarama-Muyumba-Nyagatare triangle – was relatively quiet early on, it saw most of action during mid-October. Put under the overall command of Lt Col Déogratias Nsabimana, FAR units deployed in this area included the Para-Commando Battalion, elements of the Reconnaissance Battalion, and one of newly-established infantry battalions.[81]

On 8 October 1990, the Para-Commando Battalion began an advance in direction of Nyagatare and, after being delayed by a breakdown of radio communications with its rear-base in Ngarama, took the village of Rukomo, about 10 kilometres (6.21 miles) from Muvumba.[82] On 10 October, the unit clashed with the 9th Battalion RPA, while the latter attempted to reinforce its comrades in Nyagatare. Subsequently, this small town became the nexus of a protracted battle that lasted longer than a week and during which the place changed hands several times. It was only on 16 October that the insurgents – supported by a number of mortars calibre 120mm – forced the Para-Commando Battalion and another major FAR unit to retreat.[83]

Despite the government's failure to capture Nyagatare, the conflict reached the status of a deadlock at this stage: although both sides rushed hastily trained reinforcements to the battle, neither could continue its advance. That said, although taken by surprise, the FAR reacted quickly and managed to limit the extension of the RPA's penetration to an area where geographical features – like densely-cultivated hills – offered wide fields of fire while providing minimal concealment. This meant that government forces were able to make good use of their superior firepower to decrease the benefit of extensive combat experience of insurgent commanders. It was under these circumstances, during the late October 1990, that the RPA began making liberal use of very young men, barely trained in recently-established camps and mostly still wearing civilian clothes. According to the government, these were several times deployed for frontal attacks on the FAR positions and suffered extensive casualties as result.

Victory in Mutara

Of course, following the ages-old adagio that any government force not obviously winning a war against an insurgent movement is de-facto losing, the situation appeared entirely different to many of foreign observers. Therefore, the FAR prepared its next

A map showing the FAR counter-attack against the RPA in north-eastern Rwanda in second half of October 1990.

Taken inside the same hangar at Kayibanda IAP, but showing another corner, this photograph indicates that the sole Dauphin helicopter used for VIP transport was non-operational as of October 1990 too. (Albert Grandolini Collection)

counter-offensive and on 23 October 1990 launched an advance in direction of tactically important crossroad of Ryabega, a small locality on the Kagitumba-Gabiro road, and connected to Nyagatare by a dirt road.[84]

Originally protected by an isolated company of the FAR, Ryabega was bypassed by the RPA during its initial advance and then besieged by two companies. Hinting willingness to surrender in order to prevent an all-out attack, the government garrison then entered negotiations that lasted several days. On the evening of 22 October, Chris Bunyenyezi lost patience and took a company and some support weapons down the road from Kagitumba, intending to storm the position. However, early the following morning, his three companies came under a surprise attack of FAR infantry supported by armoured vehicles.[85]

Namely, during the night the Rwandan military deployed

Two Rwandan soldiers (one armed with an FAL assault rifle calibre 7.62mm) as seen outside Kigali in October 1990. (Albert Grandolini Collection)

FAR soldiers taking a rest after recapturing Kagitumba Border Post from the RPA in late October 1990. (Adrien Fontanellaz Collection)

significant reinforcements to Ryabega and these began tracking the advance of Bunyenyezi's units. When the situation was favourable for them, the Rwandans attacked and routed the insurgents, causing them extensive casualties. Not only that Bunyenyezi was killed in action (KIA), but also Maj Narygira was taken prisoner of war (POW), and the insurgents lost one Type-63 MRL and a ZPU-4 anti-aircraft machine gun they had with them. Furthermore, the RPA then lost another top officer – Peter Bayingana – when the vehicle carrying him and eight other fighters was ambushed by the FAR while underway along the road between Kagitumba and Ryabega.[86] Subsequently, the Engineer Company of the army used tons of gravel to block the road between Kagitumba and Gabiro, while the last RPA attack from Kagitumba was easily repulsed by government troops on 24 October 1990.

Therefore, the FAR managed to conclude the protracted battles for Nyagatare and Gabiro with a single stroke, causing the RPA units in the north to disperse and withdraw towards the border, while those in Gabiro had their supply lines cut off. Indeed, when Maj Ildephonse Rwendeye's command resumed its advance on the later town – burning the surrounding forests in order to prevent insurgent infiltration attempts and cutting off their water supply as they went – it encountered only weak resistance and captured Gabiro on 27 October.[87] Rwendeye's units then continued their advance along the paved road, eventually linking with troops advancing from Ryabega area too. By 30 October 1990, the Ruhengeri Commando Battalion; the Para-Commando

Battalion; two battalions drafted from instructors for the Bigogwe Commando Training Centre and the Bugesera Education Centre; and a squadron of the Reconnaissance Battalion were already taking positions along the border. Furthermore, they assaulted Kagitumba, and captured the town with some support of Gazelle helicopters and mortars. This stroke hit so fast that the RPA failed to evacuate its large stocks of food supplies, and was only able to burn three AML-60s and two VBLs it captured during earlier fighting.[88]

With insurgents forced to withdraw into Uganda in some chaos, the October battle ended in a clear-cut victory for Habyarimana's government. Although FAR ground units did suffer significant casualties in fighting, two of most severe blows the government troops received occurred only after this opening phase of the war. On 23 October 1990, a Gazelle helicopter was shot down, apparently by SA-7 man-portable air defence system (MANPAD). The pilot, Maj Kanyaminbwa, survived the resulting crash but was grievously injured. His co-pilot, Lt Tylingire, was killed. More importantly, on 18 November, the insurgents ambushed an army convoy consisting of one VBL and two other vehicles, and killed Maj Ildephonse Rwendeye.[89]

Lessons from the October 1990 Campaign

Overall, the FAR proved a far more efficient and combat-ready force than expected by anybody – and especially the leadership of the RPF/RPA. Although so often heavily criticised by foreign observers, government's officers and other ranks proved well-trained and –motivated, and up to the task. While their tactics was often 'uninspiring', it was sound, and their troops proved tenacious in combat too. Arguably, infantry of the two hastily-established battalions was reportedly less-willing to assault enemy positions than the paratroopers of the crack Para-Commando Battalion (which gained reputation of 'never-retreating'), but this was unsurprising.[90]

On the other side, individual RPA units showed significant gaps in their combat effectiveness: units staffed with NRA-veterans proved much more effective than those staffed by barely-trained teenagers that rallied the insurgency after the start of invasion. While they all proved tenacious in combat, the insurgents were led in haphazard fashion by overoptimistic officers that terribly

A reconstruction of one of two SA.342Ls delivered to Rwanda in 1981, as seen in late 1990. This helicopter was camouflaged in yellow sand and olive green on the top surfaces and sides, and an unknown shade of light grey on the bottom of the cabin. Its sole armament consisted of two Matra SNEB rocket launchers for seven unguided rockets calibre 68mm each. Registration – 10K10 in this case – was applied in rather small black letters and digits directly below the cockpit doors. As is usually the case with French-made aircraft and helicopters, construction number (c/n) was applied on the top of the fin, below the type designation. (Tom Cooper)

A reconstruction of one of two SA.342Ls delivered to Rwanda in 1982 and 1984, based on a photograph taken in the mid-1990s at Lanseria Airport, in South Africa. Contrary to Gazelles being delivered to Rwanda in 1981, it was camouflaged in olive green overall. Registered as 10K12 (c/n 2163), this helicopter was probably the only example equipped with a GIAT M621 cannon calibre 20mm (always installed on the right side of the fuselage) – in addition to SNEB rocket launcher. Repaired, repainted and re-registered as 9XR-RAF, this Gazelle was returned to Rwanda in 1998, but subsequently crashed. (Tom Cooper)

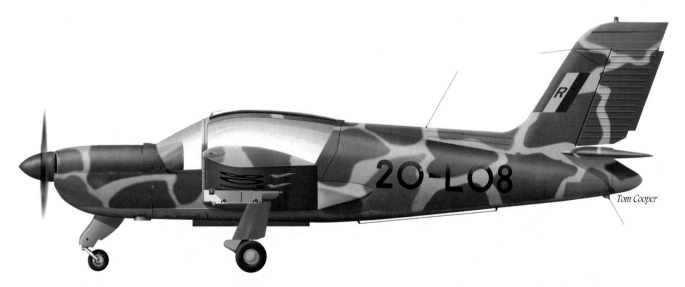

A reconstruction of the sole SOCATA R.235 Guerrier light striker of the Air Squadron FAR that remained in service until at least late 1990. As is usually the case with Guerriers exported to Africa, it received a rather complex and disruptive camouflage pattern, consisting of sand, two shades of green, and brown. According to available information, and despite being equipped with underwing hardpoints for armament, this aircraft was never used in combat. (Tom Cooper)

A reconstruction of one of a handful of FAR AML-60s evacuated to eastern Zaire in mid-1994. Rwanda received 12 vehicles of this type in 1967, and they saw intensive deployment during the civil war. All were painted in olive green overall and wore 'registration plates' consisting of their serials, and a small *tri-colore* in Rwandan national colours, on the front hull. (Tom Cooper)

A reconstruction of one of the rather elusive AML-90s of the FAR. At least 17 of these were delivered in 1986, but Rwanda might have received additional examples from France in the early 1980s; then despite the loss of about a dozen of AML-60s and AML-90s in combat, the FAR still operated 39 as of 1992. As far as is known, all of Rwandan AML-90s wore the standard, three-tone French camouflage pattern. They should have received usual 'registration plates' applied on a white field (and the Rwandan *tri-colore*) on their front hulls. (Tom Cooper)

A reconstruction of one out of about a dozen of the VBL armoured scout cars acquired by Rwanda in 1986. Like AML-90s, they also wore the standard, three-tone French camouflage pattern, applied before delivery, and 'registration plates' on the front and rear hull. Their attrition during the war was quite heavy and it seems that none were left operational after April 1994. The inset shows the reconstruction of one of few insignias known to have been applied on FAR vehicles – in this case on a VBL with registration number 8834: this was probably the crest of the Reconnaissance Battalion. (Tom Cooper)

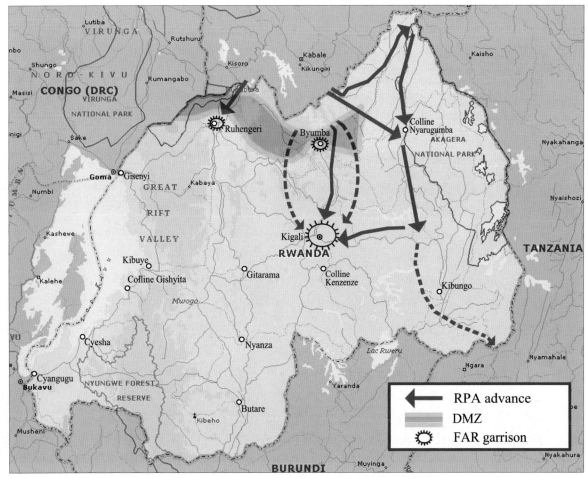

A map showing RPA's advance on Kigali and into eastern Rwanda, in April and May 1994.

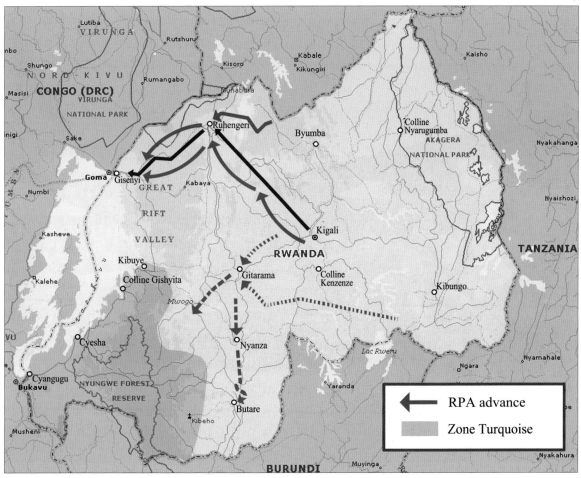

A map of final RPA's advances into north-westerna and southern Rwanda, in June and July 1994.

After establishing itself in power in Kampla, the NRA was forced to significantly expand and convert itself into a conventional military. To make for necessary numbers, it began recruiting large numbers of 'Kadogo' – child soldiers, who usually received only a bare minimum of military training. These Kadogo were photographed during their graduation ceremony in Kampala, in mid-1986. The recruitment of child soldiers became a frequent practice in several RPF-instigated wars in the DRC, in subsequent years. (Fausto Biloslavo)

Paratroopers of the 2e Battalion Para-Commando of the Belgian Army seen after their arrival at Kayibanda IAP (often mis-named as 'Kanombe Internation' at the time), together with a C-130H Hercules transport of the Belgian Air Force. (Albert Grandolini Collection)

Troops of the infamous DSP – Zairian Presidential Guard – in 1990. All were armed with Israeli-made Gallil assault rifles, a testimony of the close connections between that unit and Israeli instructors. (Albert Grandolini Collection)

A column of vehicles carrying French paratroopers waiting at the international Airport before launching another operation of evacuating expatriates from Kigali. (Pelizzari Xavier/Saviracouty Claude, ECPA-ECPAD)

FAR soldiers continued offering bitter resistance to insurgents until the very last days of the so-called '100 Days Campaign' of mid-1994. This group, armed with a Dushka heavy machine gun of Soviet/Russian design, was seen outside Kigali on 12 June 1994. (Mark Lepko Collection)

French troops with two arrested militiamen. (Albert Grandolini Collection)

One of 10 SA.330B Puma helicopters of the French Army Aviation (*Armée de l'Air de Terre*, ALAT) deployed in Rwanda in the course of Operation Turquoise, between June and September 1994. (Pelizzari Xavier/Saviracouty Claude, ECPA-ECPAD)

AML-90s of the RICMA seen under way in Rwanda. Hastily-removed desert camouflage indicates that they used to be deployed in Chad or Djibouti before taking part in Operation Turquoise – one of the last deployments of this ubiquitous Panhard design with the French military. (Albert Grandolini Collection)

A giant Lockheed C-5A Galaxy transport seen at Addis Ababa IAP, where it arrived to pick up BTR-60 APCs of the Ethiopian UNAMIR II contingent, for their transport to Kigali, on 17 August 1994. (US DoD)

As at least half the Rwandan population fled their homes, dozens of huge refugee camps emerged in south-western Rwanda – like this one near Gikongoro, seen in July 1994 – but especially in neighbouring countries. The sheer numbers of refugees overwhelmed the abilities of aid organisations to help civilians and thousands of refugees had already died of malnutrition and diseases in June of the same year.. Subsequently, many more were to be killed in the RPA's attacks. (UN)

miscalculated and underestimated their opposition.[91]

Exact number of casualties suffered by both sides remains unknown. The fact that at least 170 seriously injured FAR troops received treatment in the Kigali Military Hospital during October 1990, is not only a testimony to intensity of the fighting, but might indicate that the government lost up to 10% of its total manpower. Indeed, the RPF/RPA-leadership subsequently admitted to have suffered grievous losses during the failed invasion too.

Although badly beaten-up, the RPA did not take long to overcome its defeat. The problem of leadership was quickly solved once Paul

CHAPTER FOUR:
RE-BIRTH OF THE RPA

Kagame returned from the USA and assumed the position of the CO, in late October.

Kagame actually left the USA immediately after hearing the news of Rwigyema's death, on 8 October. Curiously, he was in no rush to return to the battlefield: on his return trip he made stops in the UK and Ethiopia, and thus arrived at Entebbe only during the second half of October 1990. Whether because he was subsequently recognised as the 'ablest' of the surviving top officers, or because he was backed by Museveni, Kagame's authority was accepted, and thus the RPA followed his order, the first of which was for its battered remnants to withdraw into the Virunga Mountains.

The march from Kagitumba to the Virunga range lasted one week and was supported by two factors: a decoy attack on the small garrison of Gatuna, which covered-up the insurgent withdrawal, and permission from Ugandan government for the RPA to make use of its territory.[92]

The attack on Gatuna was launched by a small, battalion-sized task force led by Capt Ludoviko Twahirwa-Dodo, on 3 November, and successful. However, the FAR counter-attacked later during the day, deploying two infantry companies supported by AML-60s. One of these – composed of recently-trained recruits – was ambushed on the Byumba-Gatuna road, and routed.[93]

The fighting in this area continued for several weeks longer because the insurgents made good use of the mountainous area, better suited for hit-and-run style of operations than the Mutara region. Furthermore, the FAR units were busy mopping up scattered groups of RPA that withdrew into the Akagera Park, which offered near-fanatic resistance: some of insurgents in question had to be put under siege and literally starved to death.[94] Indeed, continuous harassment of FAR units eventually enabled the bulk of the RPA to encamp in the Virunga Mountains – a range of eight major volcanoes, including Mount Karisimbi with peak at 4,507 metres (14.786ft). Except for being famous for its gorilla population, the area offered several advantages to insurgents: it was isolated, unpopulated and de-facto unassailable by the FAR, yet close to the borders between Rwanda, Uganda and Zaïre. Therefore, the RPA was in position to settle down and lick its wounds while able to communicate to the outside world and receive support without necessity to unduly embarrass its supporters in Kampala. Even so, inadequately-clothed and –fed insurgents suffered heavily in their new sanctuary: few literally froze to death.[95]

Although suffering from hardships, the RPA soon began benefitting from the political apparatus of the RPF, which very efficiently collected resources from the diaspora. Well-coordinated by Kagame – meanwhile appointed the Chairman of the seven-member High Command RPA, and Vice-President of the RPF – and his highly-efficient and parsimonious financial commissioner, Aloysia Inyumba, the fund-raising network was spreading through the USA, Canada and elsewhere in the West, providing a significant income. Additional financing came from

Kagame providing an interview to the international press after his return to Rwanda. Not the most experienced, and surely not as popular as some other RPA commanders, he still managed to impose himself as a new commander of the insurgency. (RDF)

A contemporary view of the Virunga mountain range, where the RPA withdrew after its defeat during the opening campaign of the war. (Adrien Fontanellaz Collection)

Although a failure, the initial insurgent invasion of Rwanda prompted thousands of exiled Rwandan Tutsi to join the RPF and the RPA. Most of the new recruits arrived without any uniforms or armament, and required careful training before they could be deployed in combat. (RDF)

A rare photograph taken during the process of loading the first of two Alouette II helicopters provided to Rwanda by France on 20 June 1991. The other followed in 1992. (MATAPARA Collection)

A still from a video showing FAR troops manning a roadblock in the Mutara area in 1990. Notable is the apprearance of AK-47-type assault rifles in their arsenal, probably of Egyptian origin.
(Adrien Fontanellaz Collection)

politically well-connected businessmen established in Zaire, and the Front didn't hesitate to organise 'tourist' trips into the Virunga Mountains for rich community members to see with their own eyes the poor living conditions of the frontline fighters.[96]

Fortunately for the RPF, the end of the Cold War left the Europe full of surplus armament, ammunition and equipment, offering plenty of possibilities to buy supplies at ever lower prices. Especially cash-starved countries of East Europe, deprived of their traditional customers and markets, were eager to provide most of commodities, short of most advanced weapons systems. Inyumba thus found it easy to – within only a few days – purchase thousands of very distinctive uniforms of the former East German *Nationale Volksarmee* (National People's Army, NVA), which made RPA troops easily recognisable.[97]

Nevertheless, resources obtained from the Diaspora could never have been sufficient to cover the needs of an entire army in regards of arms and ammunition. This is where Ugandan support was as important – not only in regards of provision of rear bases

for political and military apparatus, but in regards of provision of Entebbe IAP as a place for delivery of equipment purchased abroad. Ironically, the situation was further improved by the reduction in size of the Ugandan military, launched in reaction to pressure from the World Bank, which severely criticised Museveni's defend budget. Unsurprisingly, much of surplus Ugandan stocks 'mysteriously disappeared' – in RPA's depots.[98]

Even so, the RPA was never 'lavishly' equipped. On the contrary: foremost because all the supplies had to be man-handled and their transport was thus an ardous and often problematic issue, for the entire duration of the Rwandan Civil War, the Front was forced to introduce near-draconic measures to save ammunition during combat. Another symptom of this situation was that the loss of any firearm usually resulted in severe – even deadly – consequences for the responsible insurgent.[99]

Recruitment, Training and Indoctrination

Another critical role played by the RPF was to recruit, train, and provide a large number of volunteers that rallied around the movement – and were now badly necessary to fill depleted ranks of the RPA. This exiles-oriented recruitment policy was a result of very tight control exercised by Habyarimana's government but also reflected the RPA's distrust even into Tutsi born and raised in Rwanda (meanwhile designated the 'Region O' by insurgents) as potential infiltrators. Therefore, main sources of recruits remained Burundi, Uganda, Zaïre and Tanzania, with the other communities lagging far behind. Although the official ideology of the Front remained that of complete ignorance for ethnic backgrounds, majority of the Front's members remained youngster Tutsi that grew up outside Rwanda and never saw their homeland before. Indeed, one of major sources of new recruits was the community of so-called Banyamulenge: ethnic Tutsi settled in the Kivu (province of eastern Congo) by Belgians as labour force, in the 1920s. Over time these people constituted powerful and wealthy communities. They were granted Congolese nationality upon independence but found themselves exposed to increasingly violent attacks of other ethnic groups during the early 1990s. As a result, hundreds of young Banyamulenge joined the RPA: they

Another photograph taken at the same occasion (and showing this Alouette II partially inside the FAR Noratlas 9XR-GY), showing that the helicopter in question was painted in bronze green overall, and wore no markings on delivery. (MATAPARA Collection)

A still from a video showing President Habyarimana during front-inspection at an unknown occasion in 1992 or 1993.
(via Adrien Fontanellaz)

were not only to play an important role during the Rwandan Civil War, but during most of subsequent conflicts in the DRC too.

Most of RPA insurgents were well-educated: up to 20% were university-students. This proved of huge advantage for what was now a fast-expanding military service, because such a large pool of educated soldiers considerably eased selection and training of new officers and NCOs. Therefore, already as of early 1991, the RPA boasted as many as 5,000 trained combatants. This expansion was continued through 1992, by when it grew in size to 12,000.[100]

The training of new combatants for the RPA was a well-organised affair, already in late 1990. All the new recruits were sent to boot camps – such like Nakivala in Uganda – for at least three weeks, but often up to three months, before being deployed to the frontlines. Recruits were subjected to a quasi-Spartan regime, training close-order drills (with wooden sticks instead of rifles), weapons practice, self-defence, and small unit tactics all of the day. Late in the evening, already exhausted, they would receive political education courses, before getting only two or three hours of sleep. Food was scarce and their meals primarily consisting of beans and maize.

The discipline was draconic – if not outright fierce – in accordance with the RPA's Field Martial Code which defined eleven offences, including murder, rape, desertion, violent robbery and a quite wide definition of betrayal (all punishable by death). In the case of death penalty, execution was made with an *Agafuni* (hoe), in order to save ammunition. Twenty-four other offences – including drinking alcohol, consumption of drugs, or any kind of sexual intercourse (except for married men with their own spouses) – had corporal punishment as a consequence (usually consisting of beatings with wooden sticks). On some occasions the culprits would be thrown in covered and half-flooded pits. Notably, the RPA saw the application of corporal punishments as offering the advantage of making detainment facilities unnecessary, and eventually enabling culprits to return to the service. For similar reasons, deserters that were caught were beaten by their comrades – sometimes to the point of where they would remain permanently paralysed..[101]

The RPA strongly cultivated the ethic of self-sacrifice,

Troops from one of the newly established FAR infantry battalions manning a road checkpoint in Byumba area in 1992.
(Albert Grandolini Collection)

exemplified by slogans like, 'Watatu Wakikufa, Wawili Wasonge, Waliobaki Watajenga, Waliobaki Watajenga Rwanda!' (If three die, the two other continue to advance and those who survive will rebuild Rwanda!). Impressing such ideas into every combatant was the job of the Political Department RPA, which maintained the post of Political Commissar (PC) in every unit – a practice inherited from the NRA during the times of the Bush War in Uganda.[102] Like in the case of Museveni's organisation, except for being responsible for education of their troops, the PCs were also dealing with the local civilian population, but also for providing the Front with a parallel chain of information.[103]

Except for taking great care about training of new recruits, during the months after the defeat in October 1990, the RPA restructured itself in form of establishing several 300-strong battalions. Although some maintained their battalion appellation these were usually named 'Combined Mobile Force' (CMF): some were designated in alphabet pattern – like Alpha CMF or Oscar CMF – while others received numerical designations, like 11th or 31st CMFs.

A still from a video taken during the ceremony held in April 1992 when Juvénal Habyarimana officially relinquished his direct control of the FAR, and James K Gasana – newly appointed Minister of Defence (seen on the right side in suit) – took over. (Gasana Collection)

A side view of one of two Ecureuil helicopters of the Air Squadron FAR. The example registered as 10K14 was last seen at Lanseria, in South Africa, in June and July 1997. (Albert Grandolini Collection)

Expansion of the FAR

Although the war remained in the state of stalemate for most of the times, limited-scale attacks by the RPA compelled the FAR to deploy its forces so to cover the entire 250-kilometres-long (133.43 miles) border to Uganda, during 1991. Obviously, the pre-war strength of Rwandan military was hopelessly inadequate for such a task, even more so because much of the border run through the mountains. Therefore, the FAR launched a major recruiting campaign almost as soon as the war broke out, and this was followed by a massive and fast-paced expansion of available units.

Within only seven months – from 1 October 1990 until 30 April 1991 – the total manpower of the Rwandan military was doubled to 20,000 troops. By March 1993, the FAR alone (Gendarmerie not included) boasted the strength of 578 officers and 27,232 NCOs and other ranks.[104] No less but 20 new infantry battalions came into being within the same period of time, all receiving numerical (for example the 42nd Battalion) or geographic (for example the Cyangugu Battalion), or both designations (the 2nd Muvumba Battalion). Already existing units were significantly expanded too. The Artillery Battery became a full battalion of five batteries; all the infantry and commando battalions were enlargened to include one support company and four infantry companies. Some of pre-war formations – foremost the Para-Commando Battalion, Armoured Battalion, Military Police, and Presidential Guard – were held back as strategic reserve.

In order to improve the command and control over all the new units the FAR created seven operational sectors, each responsible

James Gasana talking with a group of FAR officers during the visit to one of the refugee camps in the Buyumba Prefecture in October 1992. Already at this stage, the war in northern Rwanda had generated hundreds of thousands of internally displaced persons. Notable is one of two Ecureuil helicopters of the Air Squadron FAR in the background. (Gasana Collection)

for a specific geographic area; strategic reserve units were held under the direct control of the FAR HQ, though.

Such a massive expansion came at a price. The training of new recruits was significantly reduced and largely concentrated on weapons practice. Indeed, veterans tended to call the new generation of troops that emerged out of boot camps '15 jours' (15 days) because of short duration of their initial formation. The officer corps enjoyed a somewhat better treatment but cadets undergoing training were often deployed to the frontlines in the case of emergency, before returning to their studies.[105]

Although the war against the RPA proved very bloody, the FAR never experienced problems with voluntary enlistment to fill its ranks, because it could rely on a large and expanding pool of ruined peasants and unemployed youth – all of whom were victims of the conflict. For the men in question, joining the military offered the opportunity to get a regular pay, clothing and decent food. The FAR also rationed all of its troops with two bottles of beer per day – which most of its troops could hardly ever afford in civilian life.[106]

General education level of most of recruits was low – even more so because some of local civilian administrators took the habit of 'volunteering' their young troublemakers into the military.[107] Unsurprisingly, the general level of combat effectiveness of FAR units decreased: newly-created battalions were considered of lower quality than long-existing units, some of which further lost their homogeneity as a consequence of rapid expansion too. For example, during a training session of August 1991, two companies of a newly-established battalion trained by the French had poorly maintained weapons, most of which were soon in need of refurbishment although issued only few months earlier. It often happened that different types of weapons – requiring different type of ammunition – were issued to the same company. Finally, crews of many mortars calibre 60mm were barely able of deploying these in combat.[108]

Except for the FAR, the Gendarmerie was also significantly expanded. By 1993, it boasted 6,123 officers and other ranks, best of which were organised into nine groups of approximately 250 gendarmes each, and two mobile-intervention-groups of 300 men each. All the gendarmes received basic military training and were frequently deployed to the frontline, as necessary. Indeed, some groups were equipped as light infantry formations and had a battery of mortars calibre 60mm or 82mm attached.[109]

Rush for Arms

Major factor enabling the expansion of the FAR and Rwandan Gendarmerie was the ability of the Rwandan government to quickly find new sources of additional arms and ammunition – to replace Belgium. Ties to a number of new suppliers were established already during October 1990. The first of these was Egypt with its own military-industrial complex developed already since the 1940s and offering it a high degree of self-sufficiency. The first deal between Cairo and Kigali was signed on 28 October: worth US$5.889 million, it resulted in delivery of 4,200 Misr rifles (local variant of the Soviet AKMS assault rifle), 60,000 hand-grenades, and 18,000 rounds for mortars calibre 82mm and 120mm – per four flights of Boeing 707 transport aircraft of the Egyptian ZAS Airline. Several similar orders were placed during the following years; indeed, Rwanda should have imported arms and ammunition worth US$10 million already by April 1991. The biggest single deal – worth US$6 million – was signed in March 1992, and included an order for 70 mortars calibre 60mm and 81mm, a battery of D-30 howitzers made in Egypt, 450 Misr rifles, and a huge amount of ammunition.[110]

Another new source of arms for Rwandan government became South Africa, which signed the first deal with Kigali in late October 1990 – despite the UN Security Council Resolution 558, which recommended member-states to restrain from buying weapons to South Africa (and banned their export to South Africa). This resulted in deliveries of 5,000 R4 assault rifles, 250 SS-77 machine guns, 100 Browning M2 heavy machine guns (calibre 12.7mm), mortars calibre 60 and 81mm and diverse ammunition. Most of armament in question was delivered on board unmarked Boeing 707s and C-130s, seven landings of which were observed at Kigali IAP during November 1990. During the same month, four South African instructors trained 40 FAR officers as instructors for weapons in question. Additional orders for arms from South Africa followed, so that by 29 May 1991, Rwanda received 20,000 additional R4s, 10,000 hand-grenades and 1.5 million rounds of ammunition.[111]

Other new sources of arms became the People's Republic of China, Greece, Poland and Israel. Beijing is known to have sold equipment worth US$1 million (including Type-63 MRLs and heavy machine guns calibre 12.7mm), and in total, Rwanda imported arms worth US$83 million between 1990 and 1994, thus becoming the third largest arms importer in Africa.[112] Such a massive spending was possible only through Kigali increasing its defence budget from 1.71% of the GDP in 1989, to 3.75% in 1990, and 5.52% in 1991. While part of this was financed, through the introduction of solidarity tax of 8% on all salaries, most came through lending from various international institutions

(like the World Bank and the International Monetary Fund), which Rwandans easily fooled with help of variety of accounting manipulations.[113] Overall, it was in this fashion that the FAR was expanded to the status as provided in Table 5.

Table 5: FAR Order of Battle, January 1993[114]

Minister of Defence: James Gasana CoS FAR: Col Déogratias Nsabimana
Ruhengeri Operational Sector (CO Lt Col Augustin Bizimungu)
Ruhengeri Commando Battalion
32nd Battalion
52nd Battalion
63rd Battalion
73rd Battalion
Kirambo Operational Sector (CO Lt Col Vénant Musonera)
61st Battalion
64th Battalion
Byumba Operational Sector (CO Lt Col Gratien Kabiligi)
Cyangugu Battalion
17th Battalion
31st Battalion
51st Battalion
53rd Battalion
85th Battalion
Mutara Operational Sector (CO Lt Col PHeneas Munyarugarama)
Gitarama Battalion
1st Muvumba Battalion
2nd Muvumba Battalion
3rd Muvumba Battalion
81st Battalion
82nd Battalion
Kibungo Operational Sector (CO Lt Col Edouard Hakizimana)
Huye Commando Battalion
74th Battalion
92nd Battalion
42nd Battalion
Directly Assigned to FAR HQ
CRAP (officially part of the Para-Commando Battalion)
Presidential Guard Battalion
Para-Commando Battalion
Reconnaissance Battalion
Anti-Aircraft Battalion
Artillery Battalion
Military Police Battalion
91st Battalion

French Support

While the government in Kigali began purchasing arms, ammunition and equipment elsewhere abroad, France remained the major provider of weapons and instruction. Indeed, many of most-important deliveries of arms for the FAR between 1990 and 1994 came straight from the depots of the French military.

One of most important aspects of the aid provided by Paris was ammunition. In total, France is known to have supplied 1.658.419 rounds for fire-arms calibre 5.56, 7.62, and 9mm; 132,400 rounds for 12.7mm heavy machine guns; 12,850 bombs for mortars calibre 60mm and 81mm; 11,000 bombs for mortars calibre 120mm; and 3,570 shells for 90mm cannons of FAR's AML-90 armoured cars. Another important aspect was that of weapons, which included a battery of six powerful RTF1, rifle-bored heavy mortars calibre 120mm, two launchers for Milan anti-tank-guided missiles (ATGMs), a battery of HM2 howitzers calibre 105mm (French nomination of US-made M101s), and 70 HM2 heavy machine guns. The French also provided three additional Gazelle helicopters between April and October 1992 (in response to a Rwandan order from April 1991), and two Alouette IIs, enabling their use for training purposes. The Air Squadron further received six SNEB rocket launchers and 1.397 unguided rockets calibre 68mm, plus 2.040 rounds calibre 20mm for M621 cannons of its Gazelles.[115] All equipment, spares for helicopters and armoured vehicles, parachutes for pilots and Para-Commandos, but also Rasura ground-surveillance radars, new communication equipment and even typewriters came from Paris, increasing importance of France as supplier by a magnitude: this help not only enabled the FAR to continue using French equipment acquired at earlier time, but also to improve its total firepower.

Another aspect of French aid was increased presence of advisors. The 20-man strong technical military assistance team present in the country since earlier times was reinforced in March 1991, through additional instructors attached to the Air Squadron, Reconnaissance Battalion and the Para-Commando Battalion. Eventually, this reached sufficient proportions that it received an official designation, the *Détachment d'Assistance Militaire et d'Instruction* (DAMI) 'Panda'. The DAMI Panda was initially divided into one tactical and one specialised training team, supported by command- and communications elements – with 30 men drawn from the 1st RPIMa.[116] Its primary task was training of newly-established FAR units with the aim of correcting deficiencies caused by insufficient earlier training – including unimaginative tactics (like frontal attacks), poor use of available support weapons, and reluctance to engage in nocturnal operations. It was running four-to-five weeks-long training sessions, which – for example – enabled nine Rwanand battalions re-trained in 1992 to return to the frontlines far better trained, motivated and ready to confront the RPA.[117]

The number of French advisers in Rwanda was further increased during subsequent years, reaching peaks at between 80 and 100 by 1993, of which most were drawn from French Army units. One of their greatest achievements was the establishment of the *Commando de Recherche et d'Action en Profondeur* (Long-Range Reconnaissance Commando, CRAP), a special-force-type of asset created from elements of the Para-Commando Battalion, equipped with night-vision goggles, six Steyr-Mannlicher sniper rifles, and other specialised equipment, in 1991.[118] The CRAP was assigned directly to the FAR HQ and used to infiltrate RPA lines by night

in order to collect intelligence – or simply harass insurgents with sniper fire. This unit of only 34 provided invaluable service but paid a massive price for its success: nearly half of its men were dead by November 1992.[119]

Another special-forces type of asset was created by the dedicated training cell attached to the Presidential Battalion. This was the *Groupe de Sécurite et d'Intervention de la Garde Présidentielle* (Presidential Guard Security and Intervention Group, GSIGP) – modelled after the famous French GIGN.[120] Finally, the French instructors helped create three infantry companies specialised in nocturnal operations, and a small signals-intelligence-gathering (SIGINT) unit equipped and trained to intercept and analyse RPA's radio communications.[121]

New War in the North

Aiming to achieve a notable success and show its recovered power, in January 1991 the RPA launched an attack on provincial capital of Ruhengeri, in turn marking the onset of a new phase of the Rwandan Civil War. The target it chose for this purpose was well-selected: it was not only very close to the RPA's sanctuary in the Virunga mountains, but positioned in the heartland of the Northern elites in power in Kigali, which were expected to receive a massive psychological blow through demonstration of FAR's inability to protect them.

During the evening of 22 January 1991, the 17th, Delta, Lima and Oscar CMFs RPA left the Virunga Mountains and marched by night towards their target. After the Lima Mobile positioned itself to block the accesses to Ruhengeri, Delta and Oscar attacked early on 23 January and gained control over most of the town by the noon – although not without some fierce fighting against several of bypassed FAR units that took refuge in the local Gendarmerie base.[122]

Rwandan military reacted by deploying significant reinforcements including the Para-Commando Battalion, which counter-attacked already the same day, by launching a linear-sweep from the eastern outskirts towards the town-centre. Despite the speed of this intervention, the FAR was unable to prevent the RPA from leaving the area unscathed, split into two columns and retreat into Virunga. With this, the insurgents successfully concluded their mission – which included freeing several well-known political prisoners from the local prison, but also capturing significant stocks of food, and several hundred heads of cattle. Although the FAR subsequently secured Ruhengeri, the French considered the situation critical enough to deploy two platoons of their troops to help evacuate 185 expatriates from 10 different countries, and 52 Rwandan VIPs.[123]

During the following months, the RPA continued launching small-scale attacks along the Rwandan-Ugandan border. On some days, as many as ten insurgent attacks took place, purposely scattered in time and place in order to confuse defenders and prevent Rwandan military from concentrating in one area. This forced the FAR to protect the border with a dense network of defensive positions and small garrisons, usually constructed atop

A Belgian soldier (right) in talks with an FAR NCO outside Kigali. The number of French military advisers to Rwanda was increased to between 80 and 100 in the period between early 1991 and early 1993, resulting in improved effectiveness of the FAR. (Albert Grandolini Collection).

The infamous Colonel Théoneste Bagosora (left; one of the main organisers of the Rwandan Genocide of 1994), with the German Ambassador to Rwanda at Camp Kanombe. (MININDEF)

thus preventing them from establishing 'liberated' zones. For example, when the 4th and the 9th CMFs assaulted FAR garrison in Nyagatare, in March 1991, they were beaten back with nearly 50% loss. Similarly, when five CMFs occupied several localities in the Mutara region, in July 1991, the FAR hit back with a powerful counter-attack, forcing them to scatter and flee to Uganda again.[125]

Besieging the Besieged

The absolute necessity for the RPF to finally gain a foothold inside Rwanda, and for the FAR to deny insurgents any chance of establishing presence in the country, were to dictate the character of the fighting for most of 1991. For this purpose, either Kagame or Senior Officer Sam Byaruhanga began developing new tactics, designed to overcome the RPA's main deficiency – lack of firepower resulting in inability to assault fortified positions or repulse FAR counter-attacks. The essence of what they developed was conduct of offensive operations in defensive fashion. The first solution was for the RPA units to advance into Rwanda, then entrench themselves in well-camouflaged positions and then let the government troops attack them. Another tactics they developed was called 'Cut-off': it consisted of an infiltration behind enemy lines by night, and surrounding of FAR positions with own trenches only 50 metres away in order to prevent them from using support weapons for risk of hitting own troops. Both methods were aiming to leave the government troops without a choice but to assault insurgent fortifications and pay the price for taking them.

The ideas backfired, however, then not only that the FAR quickly adapted to this new threat, but the RPA also suffered heavy losses. Namely, the government troops reacted by occupying positions around insurgents and cutting them off: left without resupply of food and ammunition, several RPA units were nearly annihilated.[126] Insurgent countermeasure was quickly developed: they would deliberately left open at least one venue of retreat for besieged garrison, enticing them to abandon their positions. By applying this tactical methods, the RPA managed to progressively gain the upper hand in the course of several battles in the Mutara region, starting with 3 October 1991.

In the course of that operation, eight mobiles preparing for an offensive against Muvumba collided with a multi-battalion FAR

hilltops – all with the aim of preventing insurgents from gaining a permanent foothold inside Rwanda. However, there was no way the government forces could have hermetically sealed the border, alone because of the terrain.

Exploiting one of such series of minor attacks, in May 1991 the Bravo and Mike CMFs marched into the Akagera Park and set up two ambushes for the FAR, killing 102 soldiers near Gabiro, on 18 and 22 of the month.[124]

Not all the action was as one-sided, however: the RPA units usually proved unable to penetrate heavily-fortified positions and suffered heavy casualties whenever trying to do so; furthermore, the FAR reacted to each incursion with fierce counter-attacks, repeatedly forcing insurgents to withdraw into Uganda and force, supported by a battery of 120mm mortars of the Artillery Battalion, and Type-55 and ZPU-4s of the LAA Battalion, and at least a squadron of AMLs from the Reconnaissance Battalion. While inflicting heavy casualties upon insurgents, the FAR suffered badly too and failed to take RPA positions.[127]

Despite this failure, the FAR regrouped and – deploying several mixed formations consisting of infantry supported by all heavy armament that was available, including AML armoured cars, clak, heavy artillery, and mortars calibre 120mm – launched a series of attacks the insurgents called the 'Rukukoma' ('composed of everything'), through late October and November 1991. Primarily because government troops had the habit of retreating back to their line of departure in the evening, all of these efforts have failed to dislodge the RPA from its positions.

Meanwhile, fierce battles were fought in other areas, primarily Kabuga (besieged for months) and the Kabongoya Hill (re-named 'Sarajevo' by insurgents). Surprisingly enough, although highly successful in spite of fierce insurgent resistance, the government troops then abandoned all of their gains by night and retreated to their starting positions. This resulted in a situation where, while suffering very heavy losses during this period, the RPA progressively began to gain the upper hand in the bloody contest and establish itself in control over minor patches of Rwandan territory along the border to Uganda.[128]

Byumba Offensive

In early 1992, the RPA renewed its attacks on border posts. On 2 January Yankee and Zulu CMFs simultaneously attacked positions in Mimuri and Nyagatare, while on 23 of the same month the Charlie, Lima and the 43rd CMF attacked several FAR strongholds in Ruhengeri area. Finally, six combined mobile forces deployed along the Muvuba River secured stretches of territory during May. Keeping in mind peace-talks scheduled to start in Paris in June 1992, and disorganisation within the FAR caused by mutinies within units in Gisenyi and Ruhengeri areas, the RPA High Command then prepared a major operation aiming to deliver a massive blow upon government forces. This offensive began on 28 May with a diversionary attack launched by Yankee CMF in Kagitumba area, while at least five other CMFs attacked Karujanga, near the Gatuna Border Post, on 5 June 1992. Meanwhile, James Kabarebe led the Delta, Lima and the 17th CMFs into a dash for the provincial capital of Byumba, reaching its suburbs on early morning of 6 June, followed by three other combined mobile forces tasked with attacks on FAR positions along the Byumba-Gatuna Road. Contrary to so many earlier cases, this time insurgents easily overcame fortified government positions, including several positioned on hills around Byumba. The tactics that made this possible was to saturate FAR positions with simultaneous attacks from multiple directions, though the insurgents enjoyed better support of mortars calibre 120mm and Type-63 MRLs than before too.[129]

The 33rd and 51st Battalions FAR, which defended the Byumba and Kivuye areas west of the road, literally dissolved under the pressure. However, early on 6 June, the FAR launched a strong counter-attack supported by artillery and quickly cleared the outskirts of Byumba, forcing insurgents to retreat into surrounding hills. During the afternoon, a platoon from the 2nd RIMa entered the city and successfully evacuated all expatriates.[130]

This onslaught by the RPA triggered a strong reaction from Paris. Eager to prevent a complete defeat of the FAR, France has meanwhile intensified its support with the aim of increasing its firepower. Between others, the French Army deployed a detachment of 25 men from the 35e Régiment d'Artillerie Parachutiste (35th Para-Artillery Regiment; 35e RAP) to Rwanda and these hastily trained Rwandan troops in the use of eight HM2 howitzers delivered recently. This battery was soon dispatched to the front and opened fire on RPA positions for the first time on 8 July 1992. Later on, French provided similar support for crews of a battery equipped with six D-30 howitzers calibre 122mm, purchased from Egypt – because Egyptian instructors deployed to Rwanda did not speak French.[131] The combination of fire-power and improved skills of government troops proved devastating for insurgents: the howitzers provided precise and deadly support, several magnitudes better than earlier 'area shelling' to which they were accustomed. The tactics of each FAR artillery battery was to first mark the targeted area with smoke shells, have it corrected by forward observers, and then lob a volley of 50 shells within less than a minute. Such barrage was often combined with fire from other support weapon, deployed to saturate the same target. Although the RPA was meanwhile very good in digging trenches, its positions proved insufficient against such an onslaught, precision of which was further improved through very good artillery control by the FAR, and it began suffering terrible casualties. Before soon the insurgents dubbed the 105mm howitzers *Dimba Hasi* ('Boom, on the Ground'). The FAR artillery proved highly effective in counter-battery actions too: it not only destroyed four insurgent mortars calibre 82mm and 120mm and three ZPU-4s, together with their crews, but forced the RPA to completely cease using heavy weapons. To add to the misery of the insurgents, Gazelles of the Air Squadron returned to action, flying dozens of attack sorties: by approaching enemy positions low along valleys before unleashing their unguided rockets, they usually caught the RPA by surprise and began delivering severe blows too.[132]

Therefore, by the time a ceasefire was effective, on 31 July, the RPA suffered not only as many as 2,500 casualties: CMFs like the 17th, Delta, Lima and Oscar were decimated and in disarray. However, while the influx of fire-power stopped cold the insurgent offensive, the FAR failed to re-take lost positions because RPA combatants that survived preparatory barrages tended to defend fanatically, had good fire-discipline and inflicted heavy casualties too. Furthermore, it became clear that after the lengthy campaign of reaction to small-scale insurgent attacks, government troops began to lose their stamina. In one case, a FAR unit stopped a well-developing attack alone because of rumours it was about to run out of ammunition. Therefore, although suffering extensive casualties, the RPA finally gained a 10 by 30 kilometres (6.21 by

18.64 miles) sized foothold inside Rwanda – something it was longing for ever since October 1990.[133]

Vicious Circle

The ceasefire of mid-1992 was generally respected for the rest of that year. The RPA was now in a position of relative military superiority – which it would not relinquish until the end of the war – but this not only as a consequence of its tactical and operational innovation: at least as important was the FAR's weakness caused by extensive attrition of nearly two years of warfare, which began undermining the efficiency of this institution. Not only the Rwandan military of 1990-1992 period, but any force tripling in size in a matter of few months – and then suffering up to 15,000 casualties (including KIA and WIA) – would experience considerable difficulties in maintaining its combat effectiveness. However, what really caused the decline of the FAR was Habyarimana's habit of favouring certain units – primarily those staffed by Northerners (usually members with connections to the Akazu, disappointed over Gasana's appointment) – regardless of operational needs or their fighting efficiency. This caused a progressively increasing rift between Northerners and Southerners in the military, to a degree where the latter began to consider this conflict a 'Northerners' war'. While foremost obvious between higher officer ranks, this rift was not as clear at the level of junior officer. Nevertheless, it caused tensions and eventually culminated in above-mentioned mutinies in the months before the RPA's Byumba offensive. While desertions were endemic already at earlier times, mutinies resulted in mass defections within newly-created units: by mid-1992, average available manpower of recently established battalions was nearly 50% below their nominal strength.[134] The situation was worsened by the increasing rift between the cadre of experienced and well-trained officers (generally considered 'good' by their French advisers, with few of them considered even 'excellent'), the 'old guard' usually assigned to units created before 1990, and those that joined the service since the start of the war. While the FAR managed to conserve the cadre of experienced officers, even elite units like the Para-Commando have suffered losses because of being constantly deployed as an intervention force. Their casualties were replaced by experienced troops from other – foremost newly-established – units, in turn weakening the latter even more.[135]

Obviously, this vicious mix resulted in an overall loss of combat effectiveness that could not be replaced with fire-power alone: not only that Rwanda could not afford buying additional heavy weapons, but it lacked qualified personnel and the necessary infra-structure to properly maintain these.

James Gasana, Rwandan Minister of Defence since 16 April 1992, worked tirelessly to improve the situation. He successfully quelled the mutinies by touring the units in question and began implementing a programme of addressing some of deficiencies by centralizing the process of officer-promotions, and reducing influence of some of Habyarimana's cronies. For example, he appointed Col Nsabimana the new CoS instead of Col Serubuga (who occupied this position since decades); Gasana stopped the expansion of the military and instead concentrated on qualitative improvement of available units; and he changed the recruitment policy to correct the traditional imbalance – which was favouring natives of Gisenyi and Ruhengeri prefectures. However, his measures proved highly unpopular within the establishment in Kigali, and – after barely surviving several attempts at his life – Gasana was forced to leave Rwanda in 1993. Unsurprisingly, after a short period of improvement, the downward spiral of the FAR continued.[136]

The ceasefire of 31 July 1992 held for approximately six months, during which the two parties became involved in protracted negotiations in the Tanzanian city of Arusha. For various reasons –

CHAPTER FIVE:
UNLEASHING THE APOCALYPSE

but foremost because of Habyarimana's delaying tactics – progress of the talks was slow.

Atrocities against civilian population were committed by both sides right since the start of the war. Early on, it was foremost the local Rwandan authorities who began mobilising Hutu farmers that instigated several massacres of Tutsi in north-western Rwanda, in January and March 1991, killing between 300 and 1,000 Bugogwe (a Tutsi pastoralist group).[137] Because additional actions of this kind followed, over 3,000 Tutsi were massacred by October 1993. This is not to say that Habyarimana officially sanctioned such behaviour (on the contrary: his involvement remains unconfirmed), nor that the RPF did not get involved in massacres. Areas that came under insurgent control were literally depopulated – partially because government propaganda prompted most of civilians to flee, but in part also because the insurgents tended to attack not only the Hutu, but even Tutsi that remained loyal to the government, considering them for 'traitors'. Most of atrocities committed by the RPA took place in Ruhengeri area in February 1993, and again in November 1993 – when a number of political activists of the MRND (Habyarimana's party) and the CDR (extremists that insisted on the 'Hutu Power' theory) were summarily executed.[138] That said, it must be observed that the RPA was much more efficient in covering-up atrocities committed by its combatants: it not only exercised very strict control over all foreigners it would left into the areas under its control, but also run any related operations by night. Foremost, the insurgents

A group of RPF insurgents crossing a river. Throughout the entire war the RPF was experiencing major problems with a lack of transportation means and often had to compensate by man-handling all weapons and supplies to the frontlines. (RDF)

Paul Kagame with his troops in 1993. (Mark Lepko Collection)

A recoilless rifle operated by RPA insurgents seen in action in 1993. (via Adrien Fontanellaz)

never claimed responsibility for their deeds. Therefore, atrocities committed by the RPA were much more 'stealthier' by nature than those committed by different Hutu militias.[139] In turn, this enabled it to use several massacres committed by Hutu from late January 1993 as a perfect excuse to breach the ceasefire with a new offensive – while simultaneously flexing its muscles in order to tip the balance during negotiations in Arusha.[140]

All-out Offensive

The RPA mobilised all of its major units for this operation, bringing about 12,000 combatants to the frontlines. By October 1992, these were reorganised: the 300-strong CMFs were disbanded and instead eight bigger formations came into being,

designated 'Mobiles'. Each of new formations had 10 companies and was at least 2,000 strong (for the insurgent order of battle between October 1992 and April 1994, see Table 6).

Table 6: RPA Order of Battle, October 1992-April 1994[141]

Alpha Mobile
Bravo Mobile
Charlie Mobile
7th Mobile
21st Mobile
59th Mobile
101st Mobile
157th Mobile

The attack began during the night from 7 to 8 February 1993, with a multi-pronged advance: the 59th, 157th and the Charlie Mobiles attacked in the Ruhengeri region, while the 7th, 21st, 101st, and the Bravo Mobile attacked in the Byumba Prefecture and Ngarama region.[142]

Some of involved units received very specific orders, like the 59th Mobile, which was tasked with destruction of the Ntaruka power station on the shore of Lake Burera, before marching for two days in direction of Cyeru, where it was to join the Alpha Mobile.[143]

The onslaught initially disoriented the FAR, especially because Gasana – who was responsible to oversee conduct of operations and whose approval was mandatory for transfer of major units from one operational sector – was in Arusha at the start of insurgent offensive. The situation was worsened by entirely new insurgent tactics: they began by-passing fortified positions and infiltrating the frontlines before appearing deep in the back of FAR units to quickly progress into the Ruhengeri and Byumba Prefectures. Before soon, battalions of the crucial Kirambo Operational Sector found themselves cut off from supply bases: they had to break the encirclement and retreat towards Rulindo, only 30 kilometres (18.64 miles) from the capital. The RPA pursued them viciously, and occupied the surrounding hills. In other areas, the insurgents managed to reach the vicinity of Tumba, mere 25 kilometres (15.53 miles) from Kigali, where heavy fighting erupted.[144]

However, the collapse of the Rwandan military was anything but universal. The Charlie Mobile met fierce resistance during its attack on Ruhengeri and failed to take the town, suffering heavy casualties while attempting to outflank the defenders. Indeed, a FAR counter-attack on 10 February forced the insurgents well away, enabling a detachment of French Army to evacuate 67 Westerners blocked in Ruhengeri.[145]

Byumba was initially bypassed by the RPA but subsequently fierce battles erupted in this area too, insurgents returning to the tactics of digging trenches close to FAR positions. Other battles erupted in the Ngarama area – where the 7th, 101st, and Bravo Mobiles operated, and where the former formation suffered extensive losses.[146] According to the French military advisers, reason for the defensive success of the Rwandan military in Byumba and Ruhengeri was very good leadership of officers in charge of respective Operational Sectors, foremost Lt Col Gratien Kabiligi and Lt Col Augustin Bizimungu. The Air Squadron FAR also played a significant role, logging 135 flight hours in 112 sorties flown between 8 and 20 February – mostly for casualty-evacuation (CASEVAC) purposes. The helicopter fleet became instrumental for delivering reinforcements, ammunition and other supplies to isolated units and evacuating wounded. However, in the course of these operations the Ecureuil coded 10K13 crashed, killing its pilot, Capt

Brigadier-General Roméo Dallaire, commander of the UNAMIR. (UN)

Two FAR soldiers evacuating their injured comrade. Notable is that although their uniforms began to differ, many members of the Rwandan infantry remained armed with FN FAL assault rifles throughout the war. On the contrary, those using South African-made R4s learned to appreciate the advantages of that type. (Albert Grandolini)

Silas Hategekimana. Contrary to earlier times, the Gazelle flew only 5 CAS missions and fired mere 60 rockets, because the RPA's new tactics of infiltration provided them with only fleeting targets: insurgents learned to dig-in very quickly when not on the move, and were generally avoiding roads during daylight.

By 20 February, the FAR had all of its strategic reserved engaged: the Reconnaissance Battalion had detachments supporting all infantry battalions around the country, while the Para-Commando Battalion played its usual role of a 'fire-fighter', but suffered heavy casualties. The CRAP was inserted several times with help of helicopters but lost its first soldier on 10 February 1993.

French Intervention

Paris reacted quickly to the RPA onslaught and took a series of steps in support of the FAR. Starting on 8 February 1993, the Noroît Detachment was progressively reinforced to full battalion, consisting of three companies the 8e RPIMa and the 21st *Régiment d'Infanterie de Marine* (Naval infantry regiment, RIMa). These were supported by a heavy mortar platoon and a reconnaissance detachment from the 1e RPIMa. Other specialised outfits, like long range reconnaissance elements from the 13th *Régiment de Dragons Parachutistes* (Parachutist Dragoons regiments, RDP) and SIGINT specialists were also in Rwanda to provide intelligence.[147] The sheer presence of the Noroît Detachment guaranteed that the RPA could never take Kigali without engaging in an all-out battle with crack French troops. Nevertheless, the French Presidential Palace in Elysée went a step further and began to provide a discreet – and highly effective – support to the struggling Rwandan military.

On 22 February, a small detachment of 1st RPIMa led by that regiment's CO, Colonel Didier Tauzin, arrived in Kigali and took control over the DAMI elements already in the country. This outfit – composed of 14 officers, 30 NCOs and 23 corporals, all very experienced professionals (all were from the 1e RPIMa except about a dozen from the 35e RAP) – was now tasked with

The HQ of the UNAMIR in Kigali, as seen in 1994. (UN)

directly supervising the Rwandan military through establishment of a parallel hierarchy.[148] Correspondingly, several officers were assigned to the FAR HQ, starting with 23 and 24 February, and began planning its operations, while three teams each of 12-14 soldiers were dispatched to assist commanders of three most threatened Operational Sectors (Ruhengeri, Byumba and former Kirambo, meanwhile renamed Rulindo Operational Sector). Furthermore, seven gunners from the 35e RAP formed three teams attached to the batteries of the Artillery Battalion equipped with HM2s, D30s and RTF-1: their presence vastly improved the already deadly effectiveness of this unit through addition of capability to hit even moving RPA formations.[149]

By concentrating its major effort on the central sector of the 250-kilometres (155.34 miles) wide frontline, the reinvigorated FAR managed to stabilise the situation in a matter of few days. Insurgent advance was stopped by a combination of better organisation of defensive positions, limited counter-attacks and the death of nearly 800 RPA combatants within only eight days. Furthermore, each Operational Sector established a small commando unit, tasked with harassment operations behind insurgent lines. Indeed, the

Ghanaian troops driving M113s of the UNAMIR II in 1994. These types of armoured vehicles were not in service with the Ghanaian Army and their crews therefore experienced some difficulties with manoeuvring these APCs properly – although Ghanaian soldiers were some of the best of this UN mission. (Albert Grandolini Collection)

Troops from the Chadian contingent that served in Rwanda during Operation Turquoise and then in UNAMIR II.
(Albert Grandolini Collection)

involvement of French advisers became so intensive, that several occasions occurred in which they had to open fire at insurgents in order to extract themselves from enemy infiltration attempts, and one of them was slightly wounded.[150]

Exploiting the defensive success, Tauzin then collected about 3,000 FAR troops to create a reserve force which he planned to use for a major counter-attack from Byumba, code-named 'Operation Miyove'. Intended to devastate the RPA and planned for 2 March 1993, this enterprise was called off by Paris only minutes before it was about to start.[151]

Instead, a new ceasefire was agreed for 7 March, leaving the insurgents as de-facto victors although heavy losses forced them to withdraw to their starting positions. Before this offensive, the RPA held only a very small part of Rwanda: subsequently, it held an area that was 120 kilometres long and 20 kilometres wide: during the subsequent negotiations, the insurgents were forced to vacate this area but the FAR was not permitted to enter it either. In this fashion, a 'De-militarised Zone' (DMZ) came into being between the government forces and the insurgents, which was obviously out of the control of Kigali too: instead, it was monitored by a few dozens of officers from the Neutral Monitoring Group of the Organisation of African Unity. Furthermore, not only that Kagame and his aides became convinced of their military superiority, but the FAR received a massive psychological blow: this reached such extensions that most of foreign observers – rather prematurely – concluded that the Rwandan military was unable to defeat the RPA on its own.[152]

UNAMIR: Undermanned, Underfinanced and Undergunned

Once the ceasefire of 7 March became stabile, the Government of Rwanda and the RPF requested the United Nations to deploy a neutral international force to Rwanda. The UN reacted by establishing the United Nations Observer Mission Uganda-Rwanda (UNOMUR), tasked with monitoring the 193 kilometres (119.92 miles) long border between the two countries with the aim

of preventing deliveries of military supplies to the RPA. However, assigned only 81 unarmed observers, this mission proved entirely futile: such a small number of men could simply never stop the influx of supplies for insurgents along a myriad of mountain trails, especially because they were not supported by helicopters capable of flying nocturnal reconnaissance missions.[153]

Nevertheless, the Government and the RPF intensified peace-negotiations and eventually signed the Arusha Peace Treaty, on 4 August of the same year. This included a power-sharing agreement and a plan for integration of the RPA into the FAR, with the latter planned as a 13,000-strong national army in which insurgent officers were to get up to 50% of commanding positions.

Between 19 and 31 August 1993, a reconnaissance mission of the United Nations, led by the Canadian Brigadier-General (Brig Gen) Roméo Dallaire, visited Rwanda to study the feasibility of such a mission and assess what means were required to run such an operation. On 5 October 1993, Security Council of the UN issued the Resolution 872, creating the United Nations Assistance Mission for Rwanda (UNAMIR), the task of which was to support the implementation of the Arusha Peace Treaty, foremost through supervising the ceasefire, but also through restoring general security all around the country, pending general elections.[154]

Exactly like the UNOMOR, the UNAMIR was to suffer from numerous flaws, some of which were to prove fundamentally damaging for security and stability of Rwanda. The first of these was predisposition that both parties in the conflict were supposed to support the UN mission and willing to follow the peace process. This resulted in the UNAMIR receiving the mandate according to Chapter VI of the UN Charta, resulting in the UN troops lacking means to impose its will upon involved parties, nor have its own intelligence service: instead, it was supposed to receive intelligence from local actors, as and when requested.[155]

The next problem with the UNAMIR was that very few of involved officers spoke any French – then the second official language in Rwanda – and even less so Kinyarwanda. This meant that the UN mission was heavily dependable upon local translators, and in turn vulnerable to leaks towards political and military actors. Another problem was that UNAMIR radio sets provided by US company Motorola, had no encryption capabilities, which meant that they were vulnerable to interception – particularly so to the highly efficient Directorate of Military Intelligence (DMI) of the RPA.[156]

Another series of flaws was related to the international situation. The UN was at the same time involved in numerous conflicts, some of which attracted far more attention than the situation in Rwanda, and drained organisation's financial resources. Therefore, while Brig Gen Dallaire considered a 4,500-strong force as necessary for the mission, he was given only 2,548. The first elements of the UNAMIR arrived in Rwanda in October 1993, and by March 1994 the mission reached its peak having 2,508 officers and other ranks from militaries of no less but 22 different countries.[157]

Financial constraints of the mission had adverse effects upon UNAMIR's capabilities too. Ammunition was always in short supply (on average, every soldier was assigned less than 100 rounds), and the force was lacking in armoured vehicles and helicopters. Although Belgians provided two CVR(T) Scimitar light reconnaissance tanks armed with 30mm cannons and four CVR(T) Spartan APCs armed with MAG machine guns, some of these were in need of repairs while others lacked suitable ammunition. Similarly, out of eight BTR-80 APCs provided by the UN mission in Mozambique, only five were in working order, while 100 pick-up trucks inherited from the UN mission in Cambodia were vandalised during the transit and only 30 were useful immediately on arrival. First two helicopters arrived only in late March 1994, and were piloted by civilian contractors who left the country already on 7 April of the same year. Therefore, UNAMIR's mobility depended exclusively on 466 SUVs and other general-purpose vehicles, and 109 trucks.[158]

As always during operations of such multi-national bodies, the capabilities of detachments from different militaries around the world varied widely. Involved officers stressed that the troop quality was good in general, although the battalion from Bangladesh was no cohesive unit, but an over-staffed march formation of men unaccustomed to work as a team that arrived in insufficiently trained condition and equipped only with their personal weapons and kit. In comparison, the battalion from Ghana was considered well-led and cohesive, as were the Tunisian Army company and a battalion of Belgian troops – although the latter was considered 'too aggressive'. Overall, the UNAMIR could be assessed as a 'good weather force' only (for full composition of the UNAMIR contingent, see Table 7).[159]

First large-scale operation of the UNAMIR was code-named 'Operation Clean Corridor' and began on 28 December 1993, when the force was tasked with protection of re-deployment of an RPA battalion from Mulindi to Kigali. Namely, in accordance with the Arusha Peace-Treaty, the RPA was granted permission to base 600 combatants in the capital to guarantee the safety of RPF politicians that were to be present there too. For this purpose, the insurgents established a new unit, the 3rd Battalion, commanded

Table 7: Main Contingents of the UNAMIR[160]

Country & number of troops	Date of Arrival in Rwanda	Notes
Tunisia (60)	September 1993	
Belgium (424)	November 1993	Named KIBAT 1 and including elements of the 1st Para-Commando Battalion (from Diest); reorganised as KIBAT 2 when troops from 2nd Para-Battalion (from Flawinne) took over
Bangladesh (933)	November 1993 – January 1994	RUBAT
Ghana (800)	February 1994	drawn from 3rd and 5th Infantry Battalions Ghana Army; named BYUBATT while based in Byumba, later GHANABATT

by Lt Col Charles Kayonga. His troops were based at the *Conseil National pour le Développement* (National Council for Development, CND; former national assembly complex) on a small hill near the barracks of the Presidential Guard in centre of Kigali. The convoy of 80 vehicles carrying troops of the 3rd Battalion and UNAMIR escort arrived at its destination without any problem – and was even warmly greeted by the local population. However, once inside its compound, the RPA troops immediately began transforming it into a fortress, including emplacements for their mortars and heavy machine guns, bunkers, and an extensive network of – covered – trenches. Furthermore, insurgents exploited the presence of their comrades inside the capital to start infiltrating their undercover elements.[161]

While the UNAMIR proved nearly as impotent in regards of controlling the flow of supplies for the RPA from Uganda into Rwanda, as in countering ever more fierce anti-UN propaganda of local Rwandan media, it also proved unable to force President Habyarimana into the formation of a power-sharing government as agreed upon in the Arusha Peace Treaty. Namely, on arrival of the UN troops, France withdrew the Noroît Detachment, leaving only a few technical advisers to continue their work with the FAR.[162] This caused immense worries within circles of Habyarimana's cronies, who began feeling abandoned even by their staunchest ally. Unsurprisingly, not only the position of the 3rd Battalion RPA in Kigali became tense, but there were soon several violations of ceasefire elsewhere along the frontlines between the FAR and insurgents. Monitoring such violations soon became the main preoccupation of the UNAMIR. Through early 1994, four FAR soldiers were killed and nine wounded, and one RPA soldier killed in two incidents in the Warufu Valley, while on 26 February a convoy carrying supplies for the RPA garrison was ambushed in the suburbs of Kigali. After the lead vehicle carrying insurgents was hit by a grenade and immobilise, the Belgian peacekeepers retreated, leaving beleaguered and isolated RPA troops behind. The unit called for help from the 3rd Battalion and this dispatched two sections that quickly infiltrated the ambush and rescued

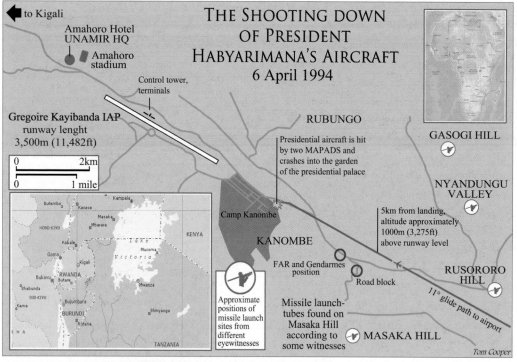

A map of the shooting down of President Habyarimana's aircraft.

Wreckage of the Falcon 50 that was carrying Presidents Juvénal Habyarimana and Cyprien Ntaryamira when it was shot down on 6 April 1994. (Pit Weintert Collection)

Two of many Hutu militiamen that were roaming Kigali during April 1994. (Albert Grandolini Collection)

their comrades, who by then suffered one fatal casualty.[163]

Overall, the presence of the UNAMIR contingent in Rwanda had rather negative than positive effects upon the progressively worsening situation in Rwanda. Foremost, it resulted in conditions where major parties in the conflict abandoned all hope for agreements of the Arusha Peace Treaty to be realised. On the contrary, through early 1994 it became obvious that the country was a powder keg waiting for a spark to ignite it.

Poisonous Cocktail

Ironically, except for the invasion of the RPA and de-facto failure of the UNAMIR, major contribution for what happened in Rwanda of 1994 was provided by political opening of the country, starting with introduction of a multiparty system. This began already back in June 1991 and almost immediately resulted in appearance of numerous rivals to Habyarmiana's MRND. These included the long-forbidden *Mouvement Démocratique Républicain* (Republican Democratic Movement, MDR), the *Parti Libéral* (Liberal Party, PL), the *Parti Démocratique-Chrétien* (Christian Democratic Party, PDC), the *Parti Social-Démocrate* (Social-Democratic Party, PSD), and the *Coalition pour la Défense de la République* (Coalition for the Defence of the Republic, CDR). Although the notorious CDR was a clearly pro-Hutu and extremist organisation, the Rwandan political scene was much more complex but to be separated along a straightforward division between Hutu and Tutsi. The PL was attracting middle-class, urban people and included many Tutsi; the PSD was foremost active in the South and included Hutu and Tutsi alike; while the MDR was largely but not exclusively composed of southern Hutu. Indeed, even the MRND was divided between a liberal wing and a conservative – and extremist – one, gathering around Habyarimana and his close associates.[164] Overall, Tutsi living in Rwanda were very far from 'automatically' supporting the RPF, while Hutu from the North were more concerned about political threat emitted by Hutu from the South – because the later were known to have traditionally been excluded from the national wealth distribution. Even such a North-South division is actually an over-simplification because the MDR had numerous supporters in the northern Ruhengeri, who felt neglected compared to more favoured Gisenyi Province... The only generalization that appears acceptable would be a conclusion that as of 1990-1992, the Rwandan political scene was comparable with a triangle, including the faction supporting the President; the RPF; and the internal political opposition – with

Pictured here are victims of frenzied mass killings that spread through the streets of Kigali in April 1994, and eventually evolved into a genocide. (Albert Grandolini Collection)

Victims of one of – far too many – mass slaughters of innocent civilians by the Hutu militia during the Rwanda Genocide of 1994. (Albert Grandolini Collection)

the latter often using the threat of the second as leverage to obtain concessions from the first.[165]

In April 1992, principal opposition parties formed a coalition government with the MRND, and – as described above – the government entered negotiations with the RPF. Immediately after it signed the Arusha Peace Treaty, the government was re-formed again: Habyarimana's MRND received 5 ministerial portfolios in the new government, the RPF 5, and 12 went to other major political parties. Similarly, MRND, the RPF, the MDR, the PL and the PSL all received eleven seats in the new Transitional National Assembly, while minor parties were attributed lesser numbers of seats. Habyarimana remained the President, but his prerogatives were significantly reduced, and were expected to be further reduced after national elections, expected to be held within 22 months after the Treaty was signed. Namely, the terms of the Arusha Peace Treaty virtually guaranteed that the circles associated with President Habyarimana would ultimately lose their privileges. Unsurprisingly, Northerners – particularly those serving as officers in the military who already felt weakened by the work of James Gasana – were fiercely opposed to this agreement, and thus it could be said that the Arusha Peace Treaty significantly contributed to their radicalisation because they were left in a position of losing everything if they would not oppose this agreement.[166]

Ironically, the RPF was not satisfied with Arusha Peace Treaty either. Although this granted it lots of political power in transitional institutions and the future military, its leaders knew they had no strong political base inside the country and could never win national elections. This was clearly illustrated in September 1993, when partial local elections were held in the DMZ, and resulted in complete defeat of the RPF.[167]

However, there were many more – and often much more powerful – factors that finally reconfigured the Rwandan political scene and threw the country into a murderous cocktail of chaos, radicalisation and mass slaughter. Most of these were only indirectly related to the above-described combination of the effects of the RPA offensive from February 1993 and atrocities against civilians committed by both sides of the civil war:

The RPA invasion and resulting war, but also assaults on Tutsi

communities by Hutu militias have caused as many as 860,000 Rwandans to flee their homes. Most of people crammed in refugee camps around the suburbs of Kigali. Left on their own device by the government they were exposed to recruitment efforts by various political parties and – usually extremist – militias.

Nearly all of major political parties have established their own armed wings. Originally, most of these evolved from classic 'youth groups', the purpose of which was to create a pool of young activists useful for the future of the party. The MDR's militia was called the Thunder; the PSD's the Liberators; and the MRND's the Interhamwe ('Those who Fight Together') already in 1991. By 1993, especially the Interhamwe – financed by public corporations and various businessmen – evolved into a para-military organisation. Position and influence of such parties grew massively after James Gasana was forced to leave the county, in July 1993. This not only enabled various political leaders of militias to activate own cells within the military – where extremist political leaders de-facto established themselves in control of such units like the Presidential Guard – but also enabled militias to grow without hindrance. Not only the MRND's Interhamwe, but also CDR's Impuzamugamibi ('Those who share the Same Goal') were vastly expanded, late in 1993, and armed with fire-arms and hand-grenades. Their training sessions were very short and limited to basic levels – militiamen learning to use machetes, grenades, bolt-action rifles and AK-47 assault rifles – and they could not alter the military balance between the FAR and the RPA, but they were to prove a true 'killing machine' when unleashed against unprotected civilians.[168]

Burundi – a traditional scene of endemic fighting between Hutu and Tutsi – was hit by a military coup in October 1993, when the Tutsi-dominated military had overthrown and murdered democratically-elected President Melchior N'Dadaye after he had been in power for only three months. When the Tutsi coup collapsed its leaders fled from Burundi: the government fled too, setting up a government-in-exile in Rwanda. In reaction, Hutu activists went on rampage, targeting the local Tutsi population before the Tutsi-dominated military launched a wave of repression against nearly everybody, plunging the country into an outright

Belgian paras – part of the UNAMIR contingent – seen in Kigali in early April 1994. (Albert Grandolini Collection)

French paratroopers (and a Belgian soldier in the foreground) evacuate foreigners from Kigali, in April 1994.
(Pelizzari Xavier/Saviracouty Claude, ECPA-ECPAD)

civil war.[169] Over 300,000 Burundian refugees went into exile in Rwanda, and their arrival had a deleterious effect upon local population, strengthening position of those advocating an all-out confrontation with the Tutsi. Fourthly, southern Rwanda – a region that was already suffering from an economic crisis since the late 1980s, further aggravated by the war – experienced two seasons of drought, in 1992 and 1993, which in some places brought the local population to near-starvation.[170]

Hutu extremists had a very efficient propaganda apparatus, including the magazine *Kangura* ('Wake Him Up!'), run by people close to the CDR and emitting the Hutu supremacist messages already since 1990; and the first private radio station in Rwanda, the Radio Télévision Libre des Mille Collines (Free One Thousand Hills Radio and Television Station, RTML), which began broadcasting in July 1993 and quickly won large audience.

Rather unsurprisingly considering this situation, not only that extremist political parties became ever more radical but even moderate political parties like the PL were soon divided into proponents of 'Hutu power' and moderate factions: extremism proved as excellent tool for the political establishment to hide the real antagonism between Hutu, and keep their followers united against a common enemy. In summary, a situation developed where political violence turning endemic was unavoidable: indeed, considering the mixture of racist propaganda relayed by various media, widespread political extremism, uncompromising adversaries and desperate population, an incredibly brutal culmination became unavoidable.[171]

Rwandan Genocide

In early evening of 6 April 1994, the sole Falcon 50 of the Air Squadron FAR, carrying the crew of three, the President of Rwanda, Juvenal Habyarimana, the President of Burundi, Cyprien Ntaryamira, and the FAR CoS, Maj Gen Déogratias Nsabimana, was about to land at Grégoire Kayibanda International Airport outside Kigali. Around 20.23hrs local time, the aircraft was narrowly missed by the first out of two SA-16 MANPADs fired at it. The second missile scored a hit on the left side of the Falcon and threw it out of control. It crashed in the gardens of the President's Residential Complex, killing everyone on board.

Twenty years later it is still impossible to precise with sufficient certainty who fired the two SA-16s. French investigations that began nearly immediately after this tragic event and were conducted by several successive judges could not definitely point at responsible persons.

Generally, the shot-down is attributed to Hutu extremists of Northern origin connected to the Akazu extremist group. However, various Rwandan Tutsi defectors from the last decade have repeatedly stressed that the interception was run by the RPA. This affair is further complicated by the existence of few other – more or less credible – theories, one of which is including even moderate Hutu factions.[172]

Whoever was responsible, it is certain that certain that elements of the FAR under the direct control of the Akazu – foremost the Presidential Guard Battalion, the Military Police Battalion, and the Para-Commando Battalion – and between 2,000 and 3,000 Interhamwe militiamen present in Kigali launched a vicious crackdown against leading moderate Hutus. They literally decapitated all of political parties favourable to the Arusha Peace Treaty, killing not only the politicians, but frequently their entire families too.[173]

Meanwhile, top FAR officers - including Maj Gen Augustin Ndindiliyimana, Col Théoneste Bagosora (one of most influential Hutu extremists and closely associated with the Akazu), and a number of other top ranks – held a 'crisis meeting'.[174] Bagosora's idea to take from civilian government by convincing officers to evince civilian authorities failed, because most of officers insisted that Prime Minister Agathe Uwilingiyimana (from MDR) was legally in the line of political succession. In the course of the meeting with Dallaire that night, Bagosora insisted that Uwilingiyimana was 'incapable of governing the nation' and that the committee was acting to contain the Presidential Guard, which he described as, 'out of control', but fact is that the process of eliminating the political establishment in Kigali was meanwhile well underway. Namely, Hutu extremists have subsequently 'recruited' a new government they could control, the so-called Abatabazi ('Liberators'), including a president from the MNRD, a Prime Minister from the MDR, and with various ministerial portfolios assigned to the MRND, MDR, PL, PSD

Expatriates boarding one of the many C-130 Hercules transports from different air forces, deployed to fly them out of Rwanda, in April 1994. (Pelizzari Xavier/Saviracouty Claude, ECPA-ECPAD)

A still from a video showing one of several CVRT Scimitar vehicles of the Belgian Army deployed to Rwanda in April 1994. (Adrien Fontanellaz Collection)

and the PDC. They also appointed Col Marcel Gatsinzi as the new CoS.[175] Gatsinzi attempted to keep the FAR out of the genocide but had next to no control over the military or other developments. He was replaced by Augustin Bizimungu, who was promoted to the rank of Major General for this purpose, only ten days later.[176] Namely, although a majority of politicians selected to form the new interim government were of Southern or Central origin, nearly all of them were close associates of leading extremist figures – most of whom preferred to remain in the shadows, and were busy imposing their genocidal agendas over the parts of the FAR and the administration that did not support them. The leading extremists were thus free to issue orders to kill to groups of Interhamwe and Impuzamugambi deployed all over Kigali, Bagosora often addressing them in person.[177]

By the morning of 7 April, the extremists began to broaden their targets and murdered hundreds of judges, intellectuals, journalists, and human rights activists. Kigali's Tutsi population came under attack as next, followed by dozens of members of Hutu establishment. By 11 April 1994, an estimated 20.000 people – primarily Hutu moderates and Tutsi – were massacred in Rwandan capital. Henceforth, the wholesale slaughter extended through the entire country and was usually committed by local population mobilised by local authorities and spearheaded by militiamen or FAR soldiers. By the end of April, over 200,000 people were murdered in all of Rwanda, and between 750,000 and 800,000 by the end of July – although precise figures remain unavailable because of the chaotic situation of those days.[178]

Most of the victims were killed in their own villages or towns, often by their neighbours or fellow villages – and most often with machetes. Elsewhere, different militias systematically searched out victims hiding in churches and school buildings and massacred them on the spot. Because of the culture of unbending obedience to authority, and because local officials and the RTML incited ordinary citizens to kill – and those who refused were murdered too – the countless Hutu civilians became involved in the slaughter.[179]

Outside Rwanda, these incredibly tragic days are foremost known for video-takes aired on evening TV-news, showing defenceless civilians – men, women, children, old and young –

being hacked to pieces by machete-tooting gangs, on the streets, in gardens, in shops, churches and elsewhere. Much less is known about resistance to the genocide. The only province dominated by an opposition party, Butare, remained relatively calm until the local governor Jean-Baptiste Habyarimana was deposed and replaced by the extremist Sylvain Ndikumana. Finding the local population resistant to the calls to kill their neighbours, extremists were forced to re-deploy FAR units and militias from elsewhere to kill the Tutsi.

Some of the massacres encountered unexpected and determined resistance by intended victims. One of the better-known cases occurred in Bisesero, in the Kibuye Prefecture, between late April and early June 1994. About 50,000 Tutsi civilians managed to organise themselves on hills around the town: the first line was composed of men armed with spears, bows and machetes. When under attack, they charged the assailants, attempting to engage them in close quarter combat thus reducing their advantage in firepower. Women were placed in the second line and threw stones, while elders remained on the top of hills to herd the cattle – which granted the survival of the community. Unable to eliminate this resistance, local authorities called for reinforcements, attracting ever more Interhamwe gangs from other regions, and then elements of the Presidential Guard Battalion. In the course of most vicious of their attacks, launched on 13 and 14 May 1994, over 20,000 Tutsi were murdered. Another 'operation' of similar kind was undertaken in the Kibuye Prefecture between 15 and 18 June.

Almost unknown in the public outside Rwanda is also the fact that the RPA began committing large-scale massacres too, although to lesser extent in comparison to government forces and various militias. Except for hundreds of retribution killings against suspected perpetrators of the genocide, insurgents began assembling civilians under the pretext of political meetings and then executing them. Overall, the RPA systematically massacred tens of thousands of Rwandans in period between April and June 1994.[180]

Last Stand of Lieutenant Lotin

Because Prime Minister Agathe Unwilingiyjmana remained one of primary targets of the assassination campaign launched on the evening of 6 April 1994, she was given not only protection of several Rwandan Gendarmes and 5 Ghanaian peacekeepers, but also 10 Belgian peacekeepers led by Lt Thierry Lotin (mounted in four Jeeps and carrying personal fire-arms only). Early in the morning of 7 April, she attempted to broadcast a speech at the Rwandan National Radio and the Belgian detachment arrived at her residence around 05.40hrs – slightly delayed by numerous roadblocks put up by different militias through the city – but this plan was cancelled because the radio station was already secured by the Presidential Guard. Later in the morning, about 30 members of the Presidential Guard supported by an AML-90 armoured car and a crowd of civilians surrounded and assaulted Belgians and Ghanaians: Uwilingiyimana and her husband attempted to flee before the UN soldiers surrendered but were later found and killed by the extremists. Meanwhile, Belgian peacekeepers were disarmed and taken to Camp Kigali, one of major military facilities in the capital. Once there, they were assaulted by enraged Rwandan soldiers who thought them guilty of Habyarimana's death because of accusations aired by the RTLM. Four Belgians were clubbed to death with rifle butts, but others managed to entrench themselves inside the office of the Togolese military observer, where another was killed by a rifle shot. Surviving Belgians were left alone for a while, as the FAR troops left the Togolese and the Gahnaians to escape, but then Lt Lotin killed one of Rwandans with a pistol he managed to keep with him, prompting an assault. The four survivors resisted until midday with help of that pistol and an AK assault rifle they retrieved from the body of the FAR soldier, until the last of them was killed by grenades launched through the windows. Ironically, Brig Gen Dallaire was informed about this drama but could not do anything to save Belgians because his troops were scattered around the capital and he was concerned that any action would repeat the Battle of Mogadishu from October 1993.[181]

Evacuation of Foreigners

While negligible against the backdrop of what was going on in Rwanda of these days, the murder of ten peacekeepers shocked the Belgian public and a few days later Brussels announced the decision to withdraw its contingent from the UNAMIR mission. Last Belgian soldiers thus left Rwanda on 19 April 1994. Similarly, civilians employed by the mission were allowed to leave the country by 9 April, while non-essential personnel was evacuated, thus reducing the UNAMIR from 2,486 to 1,705 men, by 20 April. Worst was to follow then, the Security Council of the UN then made a fatal mistake by issuing the Resolution 912 and reducing the UNAMIR to a mere 270 men, charged with continuing to broker the ceasefire and support humanitarian operations. More than 1,000 peacekeepers thus left Rwanda on 22 and 23 April 1994.[182]

While the UNAMIR was drawn down, different Western powers reacted quickly in reaction to violence that erupted in Kigali after 6 April 1994. France launched the 'Operation Amaryllis', deploying around 500 troops drawn from the 1e, 3e and 8e RPIMa and the 35e RAP, under the command of Col Henri Poncet (CO 3e RPIMa). During the night from 8 to 9 April a team of French tactical advisers already in the country was re-deployed to secure Kigali IAP. Between 01.30 and 05.30hrs, five C.160 Transall transports of the *Armée de l'Air* (French Air Force, AdA) landed there to disgorge 190 soldiers of the 3e RPIMa. They secured assembly points for expatriates around the city, during the afternoon. Two additional companies from other units arrived in the evening of 9 April and on 10 April.[183]

The first Belgian troops followed to Kigali IAP on 10 April, starting their 'Operation Silver Black', though their arrival was delayed by FAR troops that attempted to obstruct the runway when a C-130 of the Belgian Air Force attempted to land. Henceforth, the French placed one soldier near every of the FAR anti-aircraft batteries surrounding the runway with the order to shot on Rwandans if they attempted to open fire. Except for 800 troops drawn from the Para-Commando Brigade and commanded by Col Jean-Pierre Roman, Belgians deployed several CVRT Scimitar and two M113 APCs loaned from the US Army. Their task was to repatriate all Belgian citizens and other expatriates from Rwanda, and cover the withdrawal of the KIBATT.[184]

A smaller contingent of 90 Italian paratroopers from the Folgore Parachute Brigade arrived in Kigali on 13 April, while about 300 US Marines and three Sikorsky CH-53 Stallion helicopters were stationed in neighbouring Burundi starting with 8 April.[185]

These deployments were supported by numerous transport aircraft contributed by Belgium (9 C-130s), USA (4 C-130s, 4 Lockheed C-141 StarLifter, and 2 Lockheed C-5A Galaxy transports), Italy (3 C-130s), the Netherlands (1 C-130), Spain (1 C-130), and Germany (1 C.160). Furthermore, Canadians deployed two C-130s and 45 servicemen to Nairobi from where they supported not only repatriation of foreigners, but also evacuation of the UNAMIR, carrying 6.315 passengers. US transports operated from Mombasa in Kenya and Entebbe in Uganda. Overall, more than 3,000 people – including 1,500 Belgians, 600 French, 300 Germans, 250 Americans, 200 Canadians, 100 Dutch, 100 British and several hundred Rwandans were evacuated in a matter of days.[186]

Generally, this evacuation effort proceeded without problems, despite near continuous breaches of ceasefire by all belligerents, hostility of the RPF that threatened to consider Belgian and French forces as hostile, sporadic mortar shelling of the runway of Kigali IAP (in one instance an Italian C-130 was narrowly missed by a volley of 120mm grenades). With the departure of foreigners, and aside of the presence of much-reduced and powerless UNAMIR, the Rwandan tragedy unfolded without any external interference. The West clearly opted for non-intervention in a conflict then widely-perceived as a manifestation of an almost incomprehensible savagery, leaving the threatened Rwandan population on its own.

CHAPTER SIX:
THE 100-DAYS CAMPAIGN

When the Falcon 50 carrying Habyarimana and others crashed into the garden of the President's As described above, the FAR was decapitated by this strike too, then it lost its CoS, Maj Gen Déogratias Nsabimana. The situation was further confused because the new CoS, named ad-interim, Col Marcel Gatsinzi, was soon thereafter replaced by Lt Col Augustin Bizimungu – promoted to Maj Gen for this purpose. The general condition of the military was subsequently not only poisoned by political suspicions and infighting, but also preoccupation of several units with the genocide. On 20 May 1994, the interim government announced a purge of the military and blacklisting of 12 officers suspected for betrayal.[187] Overall, the Rwandan military was thus soon in very poor position to continue the war against the RPA.

By April 1994, the order of battle of the Rwandan military had been slightly modified: foremost, while the number of operational sectors was increased from five to eight, it included only 27 instead of 30 battalions, 17 of which were concentrated in the Ruhengeri, Rulindo, Byumba and Mutara sectors (for full order of battle of the FAR as of 6 April 1994, see Table 8). While partially addressed, deficiencies that have plagued the FAR already at earlier times have never been solved. On the contrary, the involvement in the genocide drew the attention of the military away from preparing itself for further fighting with the RPA, while many of its defensive positions were ill-concieved and nearly useless. Even before the genocide, many of infantry units suffered from mass desertions, aggravated by rumours of forthcoming demobilisation plans agreed upon in the Arusha Peace Treaty. Re-supply with arms and ammunition was made extremely complex because the UNAMIR denied the use of Kigali IAP as an entry point for shipments from abroad since 21 January 1994. Another problem emerged when France suspended any further deliveries, on 8 April 1994, and the UN Followed in fashion by imposing an arms embargo upon Rwanda. Subsequently, the government was forced to start using the airport of Goma, in nearby Zaire, to unload arms shipments. Two flights carried out by Air Zaire are known to have arrived there on 16 and 19 June 1994, carrying a total of 2,500 AK assault rifles, 500.000 rounds calibre 7.62mm, 46.369 rounds calibre 12.7mm and 14.5mm, 13.600 grenades of various types, and 6.624 rounds for mortars calibre 60mm and 82mm. While the transhipment of these was organised by the FAR, the military subsequently found itself in competition with militias, which took away much of newly-delivered fire-arms and ammunition, even more so because the Abatabazi government invested ever increasing means and energy into their expansion.[188]

Contrary to the government forces, the RPA was well-prepared to resume hostilities. UNOMIR observers could not prevent it from receiving supplies from Uganda (probably Zaire too), and

Table 8: FAR Order of Battle, 6 April 1994[189]

Operational Sector	Units and Notes
Gisenyi	42nd Battalion and 1 independent company; 1,055 troops
Ruhengeri	Commando Ruhengeri, 1st Muvumba Battalion, 32nd, 63rd, 73 Battalions; 4,900 troops
Rulindo	2nd Muvumba Battalion, Gitarama Battalion, 61st and 64th Battalions; 3.900 troops
Buyumba	17th, 31st, 52nd and 53rd Battalions; 3,800 troops
Mutara	3rd Muvumba, 74th, 85th and 92nd Battalions; 3,800 troops
Kibungo	Rusomo Battalion; 620 troops
Butare	no battalion assigned, only one independent company present
Kigali Ville	Commando Huye and Cyangugu Battalions
Directly Assigned to FAR HQ	Presidential Guard Battalion, Para-Commando Battalion, Reconnaissance Battalion, Anti-Aircraft Battalion, Artillery Battalion, Military Police Battalion, 91st Battalion

thus it amassed a significant stockpile for protracted operations, though early 1994.[190] While the insurgent leadership held a number of intensive conferences, their units began training in urban warfare, during last weeks of March. Finally, on 1 April 1994, all the RPA units suddenly changed their radio frequencies and call signs. Overall, there were clear signs of insurgents planning a new, 'decisive' campaign already before the start of the genocide, and in violation of ceasefire.[191]

As of early April 1994, the RPA still had its eight Mobiles established back in 1992. What was new about it was a number of specialised outfits, including the High Command Unit (long-range reconnaissance unit under direct control of Paul Kagame), the Military Police, and James Kabarebe's unit controlling all the support weapons – now including four D30 howitzers calibre 122mm acquired form Uganda, crewed by NRA-troops detached to the RPA. Large-scale recruiting took place during the 1994 campaign, enabling formation of several new units – including the 6-companies strong Simba Mobile, the 9th and the 15th Mobiles – although most of these were staffed by fresh recruits with only two weeks of training. With each of original mobiles totalling about 2,000 troops, the RPA boasted approximately 20,000 combatants for most of April 1994, while facing the FAR of about 24,000, and Rwandan Gendarmerie of about 7,000 (for a full order of battle of the RPA during April 1994, see Table 9).[192]

The plan developed by Kagame, Kabarebe, Steven Ndugute (Operations Commander RPA) and their aides, aimed at exploiting weaknesses of the Rwandan military in form of a two-pronged offensive. As first, few relatively small units were to launch attacks in the Ruhengeri Operational Sector, while major units of the RPA

Table 9: RPA Order of Battle, April-May 1994

Unit	Notes
Alpha Mobile	est. 1993
Bravo Mobile	est. 1993
Charlie Mobile	est. 1993
Simba Mobile	est. 1994
7th Mobile	est. 1993
9th Mobile	est. 1994
15th Mobile	est. 1994
21st Mobile	est. 1993
59th Mobile	est. 1993
101st Mobile	est. 1993
157th Mobile	est. 1993

Troops of the 3rd Battalion RPA sorting out while preparing for deployment to Kigali in December 1993.
(Adrien Fontanellaz Collection)

An AML-60 armoured car on the streets of Kigali in April 1994.
(Adrien Fontanellaz Collection)

Light trucks with FAR troops in Kigali, May 1994.
(Adrien Fontanellaz Collection)

were to launch assaults against Byumba and Kigali and provoke a clash with strategic reserve of the FAR. The second prong was to see lesser units striking through Mutara region and enveloping Kigali by advancing into Kibungo and Kigali Prefectures.[193]

More than ever before, the insurgents depended upon nocturnal infiltration and envelopment of their opponents at both the operational and tactical level. They aimed to infiltrate small parts of their units inside enemy positions during the night before attack, then let them lie down during the day, waiting for reinforcements, until becoming strong enough to launch attacks on their own. In order to avoid necessity of launching costly frontal assaults, each of targeted FAR garrisons was given one escape route. Support weapons were in short supply and to be used for laying down intense barrages shortly before the actual attack, or for simply harassing enemy positions.[194]

While highly promising, this tactics included at least two fundamental flaws: the necessary manoeuvring of involved units would take time to show effects and was certain to let significant contingents to escape annihilation.

Dash for Kigali

Curiously enough, the final RPA offensive was launched within hours of Juvenal Habyarimana's death, during the night from 6 to 7 April 1994 – in turn adding fuel to the fire of all those suspecting insurgent involvement in assassination of Rwandan President.

At first, there were only reports about a fire-fight between the 3rd Battalion RPA and the Presidential Guard Battalion in Kigali. This was continued well into the next day until insurgents launched a company-strong assault on Camp Kimihurura – main base of the Presidential Guard Battalion, located mere 500 metres (546 yards) from the CND – supported by machine guns and mortars. The 3rd Battalion rapidly expanded the area under its control: during the afternoon it reached the vicinity of Hotel Meridian and advanced in direction of Grégoire Kayibanda IAP, about 2 kilometres (2.187 yards/1.24 miles) from its base.[195]

The FAR reacted in force only on 8 April, when the Presidential Guards Battalion managed to repulse the attack on its base, while

the Para-Commando Battalion repulsed the advance on the IAP and recaptured the Remera Market. Meanwhile, the 61st Battalion – usually attached to the Rulindo Operational Sector – was re-deployed and entrenched along the Kigali-Byumba Road, north of the capital, in order to face insurgent units reported there during the night from 7 to 8 April by the Cyangugu Battalion. Obviously facing impossible odds, the 3rd Battalion then withdrew into the CND and began strengthening the perimeter around it.[196]

Meanwhile, the RPA launched its general offensive – also in the evening of 6 April 1994. The Alpha Mobile – followed by the Bravo, major parts of the 59th and 101st Mobiles, and the Military Police Unit – advanced straight for Kigali, attempting to relieve the isolated 3rd Battalion. By the morning of 10 April, after marching over 60 kilometres in three days, its advance elements reached the centre of capital, and established a corridor connecting Kigali with Mulundi. Elements of the Huye Battalion FAR counter-attacked nearly immediately, but were repulsed. Nevertheless, insurgent attacks on the bases of the Military Police Battalion and the main base of Rwandan Gendarmerie were repulsed too – foremost thanks to timely arrival of two companies of the Huye Battalion.[197]

At dawn of 11 April, a company of the 59th Mobile managed to capture Mount Rebero – highest geographic feature around Kigali – after overcoming feeble resistance of the crew of a single anti-aircraft cannon that defended it.[198] The FAR counter-attacked this position with two infantry companies of the 1st Muvumba Battalion and a squadron of AML-90s, opening a battle that was to last for several days. Although the 59th Mobile suffered at least 300 KIA by 19 April, and in spite of desperate efforts of government troops, all attempts to retake Mount Rebero ended in a failure. Insurgent resistance was not only fierce but bitter too: at one point in time, nearly overwhelmed, the CO of the RPA unit issued the order for all of the WIA that could not walk to be killed by hand-grenades. Only the arrival of reinforcements in form of elements of the 3rd Battalion saved the situation – and the life of wounded insurgents.

Meanwhile, in the northern outskirts of the city, the 1st Muvumba Battalion was ambushed while advancing to reinforce the 61st Battalion and Gendarmes defending Mount Jali, while other units of the RPA began exercising pressure upon FAR units entrenched around the Nyabugogo crossroad, which connected Kigali with Byumba, Gitarama, and Ruhengeri.[199]

RPA's Masterstroke

While the FAR was thus distracted by the RPA's advance into Kigali, other insurgent units – foremost the Charlie Mobile – opened their attacks into the Ruhengeri and Rulindo Operational Sectors. Although these did not prove threatening enough to prevent the FAR HQ from withdrawing the 1st Muvumba Battalion into the capital, they did tie down significant government forces in this area – and that until the very end of this phase of the war.[200]

The task of capturing Byumba fell to the 21st Mobile, reinforced by companies from the 59th and 101st Mobiles, and commanded by nobody less but Steven Ndugute. Following the newly-developed tactics, the 21st infiltrated and encircled the town, but did not attempt any large-scale attacks before 12 April 1994. Once everything was in place, a combined assault supported by infiltrated troops was launched, but this was repulsed by government forces under the command of Col Juvenal Bahufite. Subsequently, Bahufite launched several forays against insurgent lines of communication with Kigali, greatly disturbing their operations in the capital.[201]

This resulted in the High Command RPA bringing the decision to hasten the capture of northernmost bastion of the FAR. Here it was their superior SIGINT capabilities that proved their worth. Namely, on 18 April, the insurgents have captured Rutare, a small place near the Kigali-Byumba Road, thus cutting off the garrison in Byumba from the outside World. The FAR HQ then sent a message to Bahufite to withdraw from the town, but this was intercepted by the RPA, and insurgents quickly moved Ndugute's units – supported by Kabarebe's support weapons – into an ambush position. This resulted in a two-days long running battle in which government forces suffered extensive casualties, although they eventually did manage to extract themselves into Rulindo

Operational Sector. With its task completed, the 21st Mobile was re-directed into Kigali, where the insurgents concentrated no less but six of their major units by the end of April.[202]

The loss of Byumba was further aggravated by an intelligence disaster that happened when the vehicle carrying Lt Col Bahufite's aide-de-camp was ambushed by combatants of the 59th Mobile. In this fashion, the insurgents came into position of detailed maps of FAR positions, order of battle, all callsigns, frequencies and ciphers of the radio network. Henceforth, the RPA was able to intercept nearly all of government's military radio communications.[203]

Conquest of Eastern Rwanda

On 8 April 1994, the 7th and 157th Mobile opened their advance into eastern Rwanda by an attack into the Mutara Operational Sector. When the 157th was identified as advancing on Ryabega crossroad, the interim CO of the FAR troops in this area, Maj Emmanuel Habyarimana, ordered his units to withdraw towards Rwamagana. Following retreating government units, the insurgents then quickly overrun Gabiro and the HQ Mutara Operational Sector, on 9 April, establishing themselves in control over the entire border to Uganda.[204]

Meanwhile, other elements of the 7th and 157th Mobile converged on the town of Rwamagana, which was captured on 27 April despite fierce resistance. The FAR deployed several companies to reinforce the hard-pressed defenders, but most of these were caught in an ambush set up by the 7th Mobile while still in their busses, and nearly annihilated. The 157th Mobile then continued its advance on Sake and – after crushing resistance of various FAR units, including the depleted 31st and 52nd Battalions, supervised by Maj Gen Bizimungu – captured The Rusomo Border Post on 30 April. In this fashion, land communications between Kigali and Tanzania were cut off too.[205]

After this defeat, remaining government units in the Mutara Operational Sector refused to fight and literally melted away, leaving insurgents free to capture Kibungo, in early May. The RPA subsequently slowed down its advance in this part of Rwanda: by deploying only two Mobiles for this purpose, it had conquered nearly half of the country in less than a month, but was overstretched and short on supplies. However, left without any reserves and exhausted, the FAR had no other choice but to wait for the final onslaught on Kigali either.[206]

Battle for Kigali

Amid general chaos, mass-slaughter of civilians and continued fighting between FAR units and the RPA inside the capital, the Government of Rwanda left the city and established itself in the Gitarama Prefecture, on 12 April 1994. Meanwhile reinforced by units re-routed from Byumba area, the RPA then launched a new series of attacks. The 101st Mobile attacked the Gendarmerie contingents on Mount Jali, and captured this feature in the course of pitched battles fought between 14 and 20 April.[207]

One of crucial reasons for this loss was the fact that the FAR fire-power in the capital greatly diminished by 20 April. Namely, after firing last rounds of available ammunition, the batteries equipped with HM2s and D30s were withdrawn towards Gisenyi. The following day, Maj Gen Bizimungu – certainly one of most energetic (and hard-line) FAR officers – took over as a new CoS and ordered the CO of the Rulindo Operational Sector to launch a counter-attack on Mount Jali: after three days of fierce fighting this attack failed to make any progress. Furthermore, the Rulindo Operational Sector was meanwhile forced to relinquish control over all the units of the former Byumba Operational Sector because these were re-deployed in eastern Rwanda.[208]

Nevertheless, Bizimungu's appointment as the CoS FAR had a marked effect upon morale and combat effectiveness of the military and Gendarmes in general. For example, although Camp Kami was finally overrun by the RPA, the Military Police Battalion remained intact and managed to extract itself through enemy lines. Furthermore, when the 7th Mobile – which advanced along the Kigali-Rwamagana-Kayonza Road – arrived in vicinity of Grégoire Kayibanda IAP and Camp Kanombe, it was stopped cold by battalions withdrawn from Byumba Operational Sector that prepared very good defensive positions.[209] Elements of the 7th, 21st and the 59th Mobiles were thus forced to advance along surrounding hills and slowly box the FAR units defending the area until these were nearly surrounded, during early May. Exhausted and trying to regroup, both sides meanwhile made extensive use of mortars to hit each other: the FAR heavily bombarded the 3rd Battalion entrenched at the CND, while the RPA hit back by mortaring different military bases around the city.[210]

The stalemate was broken only during the second half of May, when insurgents managed to cut off the land connection between Kigali and Rulindo, and repulsed few weak FAR counter-attacks. On 19 May, the FAR units beleaguered at Camp Kanombe decided to launch a break-out attempt. They successfully extricated themselves to the Kicukiro Technical School and regrouped: the Military Police Battalion took the vanguard, while the Para-Commando Battalion took the rearguard, and then the column advanced in direction of Gikando, during the night from 20 to 21 May. However, perfectly aware of their plan because it was intercepting nearly all of government's radio traffic, the RPA amassed its heavy weapons and put all the nearby units on alert. Therefore, the FAR column – encumbered by a mass of dozens of thousands of civilians – found itself on the receiving end of heavy and precise mortar fire. The breakthrough was launched in early hours of 21 May and was largely successful, although thousands of troops and accompanying civilians were killed in the process. About 800 soldiers and several thousands of members of their families failed to escape and – closely pursued by RPA – surrendered to the UNAMIR troops stationed at the Grégoire Kayibanda IAP.[211]

The insurgents suffered heavy losses during this battle too, then other FAR units held their positions. Indeed, simultaneous RPA attacks on Mount Butamwa and downtown Kigali were repulsed – with dreadful casualties: one of 59th Mobiles's columns lost 50% of its troops during that assault.[212]

Bloody Siege

The battle of Kigali was continued into late May, by when it became obvious that the FAR was about to lose the war. Although still offering fierce resistance and launching numerous counter-attacks, government units became more prone to panic – especially at first signs of insurgent infiltrations or appearance in their flanks or backs. This problem was compelled by low quality of hastily trained recruits, used to fill the ranks of units that suffered extensive losses, and an outright break-down of the FAR's logistics, which resulted in units regularly running out of ammunition and supplies. The Abatabazi Government attempted to reverse the situation by throwing several gangs of Interhamwe armed with machete, spears and bows into the battle, but thousands of them were massacred by battle-hardened RPA in the course of suicidal assaults launched in the first half of June, without achieving any positive results. Finding no other solution, the FAR then began establishing small companies through combining 100 militiamen with up to 10 regular soldiers. However, by then it was too late and most of the militias began to panic and flee in direction of Gitarama. Those FAR units left in Kigali area as of the time held out, and thus the siege of the city was continued into mid-June 1994.[213]

Having recognised that the battle turned into a bloody slugfest that ate most of six of its Mobiles, the RPA sought the ways to re-start mobile warfare in order to decrease its losses, and continue envelopment of Kigali on operational level. However, battles of attrition were unavoidable then the remnants of the FAR were still holding out. On 15 June 1994, an insurgent company was infiltrated through positions of the 17th Battalion near Mount Kigali by night, and then entrenched mere 500 metres from the positions of the Huye Commando Battalion. Deploying about 100 fresh recruits led by veteran commandos and supported by accurate fire from mortars calibre 82mm, the FAR reduced the insurgents, forcing them to retreat: it subsequently retrieved the bodies of about 60 RPA combatants – primarily killed by mortar fire – while losing 10 own troops KIA. Meanwhile, another RPA company infiltrated enemy lines to rescue about 600 Tutsi civilians that found refugee in the Sainte Familie Church, and extract them with support from artillery.[214]

A fierce, ten-days-long battle was fought in Nyamirambo area too, where the 52nd and 53rd Battalions FAR found themselves so short on ammunition that they began to use home-made grenades.[215]

During the second half of June, the RPA finally captured Mount Mburabaturo in a day attack, only to be expelled by a desperate FAR counter-attack involving units staffed by fresh recruits. However, the insurgents then launched an all-out assault on Mount Kigali and overrun about 300 government troops entrenched there – although at a cost of severe casualties.[216]

Operation Champagne

With the Battle of Kigali de-facto ending in a stalemate, the RPA High Command finally found a solution on 24 May 1994, when

RPA insurgents entering Gitarama in June 1994. The first in the column is carrying an R4 assault rifle, made in South Africa. While this was probably captured from the FAR, rumours were circling in Rwanda already at the time about the acquisition of such weapons from South Africa via Uganda. (Albert Grandolini Collection)

Paul Kagame with his top officers shortly after the successful conclusion of the civil war in which he led the RPA to victory. (NakedChiefs)

A group of Hutu militiamen captured by the RPA insurgents. Many of them subsequently 'disappeared'. (Albert Grandolini Collection)

A still from a video of FAR troops fleeing Rwanda in the direction of Zaïre on a civilian truck, together with a column of several thousand refugees. (Adrien Fontanellaz Collection)

the 157th Mobile launched advance of Gitarama. The 59th Mobile – reinforced by elements of the 101st Mobile – followed in its wake a few days later. In Mugina, half-way between Kigali and Gitarama, three companies of the 101st infiltrated and overpowered a combined force of the FAR and Interhamwe and took this important road junction, albeit suffering heavy casualties again, on 29 May.[217] Meanwhile, the 157th Mobile's attack on Kabgayi was beaten back by stubborn resistance of the local garrison entrenched on Fatima Hill, and forced to bypass this town. By 6 June 1994, the RPA concentrated all the elements of these three Mobile Forces and launched an all-out attack on Gitarama and three hills around the town. Several of major fortifications changed hands number of times before the town was finally secured, on 13 June – though not before the FAR garrison suffered grievous losses and then withdrew along a corridor purposely left open by insurgents exactly for this purpose. For the rest of the month, badly depleted 157th Mobile – reinforced by the newly-established 15th Mobile – continued operations in southern Rwanda, concluding these with the capture of Butare, on 3 July 1994.[218]

With this, the situation became nearly untenable for remaining defenders of Kigali. They were still in control of most of the city, but completely isolated and without hope of receiving reinforcements of being resupplied. On 1 July 1994, the FAR therefore issued the order for 'Operation Champagne': a breakthrough attempt of all remaining units through a narrow corridor between the Nyabarongo River and the RPA-held Shyorongi Ridge in direction of the Rulindo Operational Sector. Dozens of thousands of civilians decided to join the military.[219]

The insurgents learned about this intention thanks to their superior SIGINT-capabilities and began fierce bombardment of the corridor from Mounts Jali, Rebero and Kigali. Thousands of civilians were killed before the near-rout caused the massive column to run in direction of Ruhengeri – with Bravo and the 9th Mobiles in hot pursuit. Involved FAR units retained their cohesion and repeatedly ambushed the pursuers, causing them severe casualties. This forced the insurgents to outflank the column and – after receiving reinforcements in form of Charlie Mobile – advance directly on Ruhengeri, which they secured on 14 July. The RPA subsequently regrouped its units in the area: the Charlie and the 9th Mobiles, supported by Kabarebe's Support Weapons Unit, and followed by the Bravo and the 7th Mobiles, advanced down the road to Gisenyi. They secured the town on 17 July, but only after another fierce and costly battle with the FAR in Mukami area.[220] With this, the insurgents de-facto put an end to the Rwandan Civil War. Two days later, the RPF swore its own government in Kigali.[221]

According to the US military attaché assigned to the US Embassy in Kinshasa, who was present in Goma at the time, between 20,000 and 30,000 FAR troops crossed the border to Zaïre in a large masse but relatively good order, during the second half of July 1994. Most of them walked in formation, some towing several Type-55 anti-aircraft guns of the LAA Battalion, but a few managed to bring intact AML armoured cars with them too.

The arrival of French troops assigned to the Operation Turquoise was initially warmly welcomed by many Rwandans – including elements of the FAR – who expected their allies to support them in the war against the RPA. This boy was photographed while distributing French and Rwandan flags between the government's troops.
(Albert Grandolini Collection)

The realisation that the French troops would not support the FAR, but even began disarming them and various militias, resulted in several mass anti-French demonstrations, including this one in the Kagonza area in June 1994. (Albert Grandolini Collection)

Because of such reports, and despite the FAR's defeat and retreat, what will soon be called the 'ex-FAR' was considered a cohesive force, indeed far more potent than various FAZ units present in the Kivus (like the 31st Parachute Brigade).[222]

Operation Turquoise

The reason why the Rwandan Civil War is considered as having ended with the RPA's capture of Gisenyi is that although there was still a significant part of south-western Rwanda not under their control, Kagame's men were out of position to march into this area. Reason for this inability was appearance of strong contingents of the French military in this area.

The prequel to this French deployment was delivered by the fact that ever since the RPA's general-offensive of April 1994 – and motivated as much by the 'Hutu Power' propaganda as by news about atrocities committed by the RPA – several huge groups of refugees began to leave Rwanda. According to the UNHCR, no less but 1,244,000 Rwandan refugees were registered in Zaire, and 577,000 in Tanzania by mid-November of the same year (where most of them arrived in time between May and July).[223]

Although it is meanwhile nearly certain that the US intelligence community was well-informed about developments in the country, the international community was initially flabbergasted by the 'sudden' outbreak and the sheer scope of violence in Rwanda. The UN was slow in realizing the scale of the Genocide and it took the Security Council until 17 May 1994 to issue the Resolution 918, which called for a massive build-up of the UNAMIR to 5,500 troops in five battalions, including two motorised units supported by M113 armoured personnel carriers.[224] Everybody was aware that such a contingent would take months to deploy in the country, and therefore France volunteered to deploy own military into Rwanda in order to buy time for the UN. This proposal was accepted by the Security Council UN, which – by adopting the Resolution 929 on 22 June 1994 – authorised the French military deployment to Rwanda for duration of two months under the Chapter VII of the UN Charta.[225]

Until recently, motives of the government in Paris to launching the resulting 'Operation Turquoise' were a subject of near cease-less debate – at least in France. Namely, as of 1994, French policy-making was a subject of contradicting perspectives advocated by three entirely different political groups, all of which were a part of the government of President Mitterrand, which in turn was facing presidential elections in 1995.[226] Operation Turquoise thus came into being as a compromise between these different political circles and their interests: its main purpose was of humanitarian nature, but its secondary purpose was a public-relation exercise intending to improve standing of the government at the time it was receiving bad press because of its support for Habyarimana's government.[227]

Because of a serious risk of a confrontation with the RPA, the French politicians took steps to provide the force deployed into Rwanda with significant fire-power. Indeed, related contingency planning included provision of support through four SEPECAT Jaguar fighter-bombers based at Bangui IAP, in Central-African Republic (CAR), but also four Dassault Mirage F.1CT and four Mirage F.1CR fighter-bombers that could be deployed at Kisingani in Zaïre, if necessary.[228] After meeting RPA-commanders in order to draw a 'Red Line' over which the insurgents were not supposed to advance, the French put their forces into motion with help of 2 Boeing KC-135FR tankers, 16 C-130 and C.160, and 2 CASA CN.235 transports. Chronical lack of heavy transport aircraft necessitated chartering of one Airbus, one Boeing 747 and two Antonov An-124 civilian transports. These aircraft were used to deploy 8,000 tons of supplies and 700 vehicles, eight Aérospatiale SA.330B Puma and SA.342 Gazelle helicopters to Goma, in eastern Zaïre.[229]

The first contingent of the ground troops involved in the Operation Turquoise included 222 men from various special forces units, including the 1e RPIMa, the 13er RDP, *Groupement de Sécurité et d'Intervention de la Gendarmerie Nationale* (National Gendarmerie Security and Intervention Group, GSIGN), the *10e Commando Parachutiste de l'Air* (10th Air Force Para-Commando; CPA) of the AdA, and the commando *Trépel of the Marine Nationale* (National Navy). After arriving at Goma on 20 June 1994, these were formed into three detachments – codenamed Diego, Omar and Thibaut (after pseudonyms of their respective COs), and 43, 44 and 58 men strong, respectively.[230] Advancing into southwestern Rwanda, they established a 15 kilometres (9.32 miles) wide corridor between Cyangugu and Kibuye, and secured the Cyangugu airfield, by 23 June.

Five days later, the French began deploying 3,000 troops from more conventional units, led by Gen Jean-Claude Lafourcade, tasked with establishment of a French-controlled 'Zone Turquoise' that covered the Kibuye, Cyangugu, and Gikongoro Prefectures.[231]

The northernmost part of this zone, the Kibuye area, was covered by a combined force including two squadrons of the *Régiment d'Infanterie Chars de Marine* (Naval Infantry Tank Regiment, RICM) under the command of Col Patrice Sartre, one battery of RTF1 mortars calibre 120mm from the *11e Régiment d'Artillerie de Marine* (RAMa), and contingents of troops from Egypt, Guinea-Bissau, Mauritania, Niger, Senegal, and Congo-Brazzaville.[232]

The force consisting of one infantry company from the 13e *Demi-Brigade de la Légion Étrangère* (13th Half-Brigade of the Foreign Legion, 13e DBLE), one infantry company from the 2e REI and a CRAP group from the 2e REP, and a company of Chadian troops – all under the command of Col Jacques Hogard – was in control of the Cyangugu area.[233]

This deployment of thousands of crack French troops and their allies into the heart of Africa not only reassured African governments allied with Paris (many of which felt insecure about earlier security guarantees provided by France), but also imposed a significant obstacle for the RPA. Already significantly weakened from the final campaign to conquer Rwanda, and fearing a repetition of the French intervention from February 1993, the insurgents preferred to be 'preoccupied elsewhere'. Instead of confronting the French and allies, upon hearing about the onset of Operation Turquoise they accelerated mopping-up operations against remaining FAR forces and militias. Further in the rear, several of their newly-established units continued committing 'retributional' atrocities against civilian population, while the leadership of the RPF was busy establishing itself in power in Kigali.[234]

Early during the Operation Turquoise, the French troops were warmly received by the local authorities, which expected them to fight against the RPA. All such hopes were quickly dampened when the newcomers began confiscating weapons from retreating FAR soldiers and – foremost – thousands of scattered militiamen. Indeed, on 17 July 1994, the French expelled a convoy carrying ministers of the Interim Government escorted by survivors of the Presidential Guard FAR from Cyangugu. Nevertheless, elements of the Operation Turquoise also became involved in a number of minor incidents with the RPA, with which the French maintained rather 'cold' relations. A patrol of French troops was captured and briefly held by insurgents in early July, but quickly released, and a convoy of two Peugeot P4 Jeeps crewed by troops from the 1e

Troops of the 11e RAMa preparing positions for their RTF1 mortars calibre 120mm. Manufactured by Thomson-Brandt, the RTF1 is widely used by many militaries around the world – often even in place of 105mm towed artillery. (Albert Grandolini Collection)

Once the RPA established itself in power, old friends Yoweri Museveni, President of Uganda (left) and Paul Kagame, President of Rwanda forged, an alliance that would play the dominant role in the future of the of central Africa during the early part of the 21st Century. (UN)

RPIMa was shot at by the RPA and one soldier injured, in early July 1994.[235]

On 3 July, a combined detachment of 58 operators from the 1e RPIMa and Navy commandos evacuated a convoy of 50 vehicles carrying 600 civilians from Butare, hours before that town was overrun by the 157th Mobile. Few kilometres outside the town, they run into RPA elements marching along the same road and there was some exchange of fire, but nobody was injured.[236] Another series of incidents occurred two weeks later when, on 16 July, elements of the 1st Squadron RICM became involved in a fire-fight with one of RPA's Mobiles, supported by ZPU-4s and mortars. Only a day later, a platoon of two P4s and two AML-90s clashed with an RPA-column on the fringes of the Zone Turquoise and became involved in a fire-fight that lasted well into the night. When the French were reinforced by a second platoon, around 21.00hrs that evening, they found themselves on receiving end of fire from mortars calibre 81mm and then an infiltration attempt of insurgents. Supported by AML-90s and mortars from nearby outposts, the French repulsed this attack, causing 19 casualties to the RPA.[237] The same day, AdA fighter-bombers made a demonstration flight over Giseny, to cool down the crew of an insurgent mortar battery from the 7th Mobile that began shelling the area around the Goma IAP, and subsequently the situation cooled down.[238]

During their two-months deployment to Rwanda, the French troops stabilised the 4,500 square kilometres (2.796 square miles) large Zone Turquoise sufficiently to prevent further flight of its population of nearly three million (nearly one third of them were already internally-displaced persons). Furthermore, they saved between 10,000 and 15,000 Tutsi from the genocide. But foremost, the French intervention significantly contributed to the mobilisation of international forces in reaction to the immense humanitarian crisis that developed after the outbreak of Cholera and Dysentery epidemics in refugee camps in eastern Zaïre – that killed as many as 50,000.[239] The last French troops left Rwanda on 22 August, after being relieved by the UNAMIR II.[240]

Never-ending War

While the Operation Turquoise thus represented something like the closing chapter of the Civil War of 1990-1994, this conflict – and especially the genocide of 1994 – had lasting and profound impact not only upon Rwanda, but its neighbours too. Dozens of thousands of civilians were subsequently massacred by RPA in Rwanda, while the pervasive use of war rape by Hutu extremists during the Genocide resulted in widespread HIV infection. The country was severely depopulated and infrastructure completely ruined. Nevertheless, the new, RPF-controlled government in Kigali invaded Zaïre with the aim of 'spontaneously repatriating' nearly 2 million of refugees that gathered in the Kivus anticipating RPA's retaliation, in 1996. When this operation partially failed – foremost because the instigators of the genocide fled ever deeper into central and then western Zaïre, followed by the mass of refugees – Kigali, in cooperation with Uganda and Angola, launched a military operation that resulted in the I Congo War, which culminated in removal of Mobutu Sesse Seko from power in Kinshasa, in May 1997. Mobutu was replaced by RPF's ally Laurent Kabila, who renamed the country the Democratic Republic of the Congo (DRC), but otherwise began to antagonise the Rwandans, prompting them to re-invade the DRC, in August 1998 – once again in cooperation with Uganda. This caused the II Congo War, which lasted from 1998 until 2003, and resulted in more than 5 million of deaths. Considering continuous political repression of all opposition inside Rwanda – even assassinations and hijackings of exiled Rwandans abroad – and continuous armed struggle between the Rwandan government and various of its opponents by the means of proxy-groups (like the M23 rebellion in the DRC, from 2003 until 2013) conclusion is on hand that the Rwandan Civil War never really ended.[241]

(Endnotes)

1. Chrétien, pp134-136 & Rusagara, p55
2. Chrétien, p221; Lefèvre, p17 & Rusagara, pp66-67; Notable is that Belgians used the German designation 'Ruanda-Urundi' early on too.
3. Lefèvre, pp18-25
4. Braeckman, p27; Chrétien, pp72-74; Lefèvre, p16; Prunier, *The Rwanda Crisis*, pp26-27; Rusagara, pp34-35
5. Prunier, *The Rwanda Crisis*, pp44-49
6. Braeckmann, p48, Prunier, *The Rwanda Crisis*, pp51-54
7. This sub-chapter is based on Chrétien, p137; Lefèvre, pp28-36, 39, 67-76, 150-151; Péries et all, pp98, 109-115; Rusagara, pp35-36, 43-48, 62-71, 112-124, 157
8. That said, the term Inyenzi could have been used by Inkotanyi too, allegedly because they were proud of their supposed capability to appear and disappear unobserved.
9. Between Belgian soldiers killed in Rwanda was the crew of two flying an Aérospatiale SE.3130 Alouette II helicopter, which crashed into Lake Tanganyka, in 1960. The crew of another Alouette II escaped a similar fate when their helicopter crashed near a group of Hutu activists it attempted to dissuade from attacking a Tutsi village, in the same year. Ironically, they were rescued by the same militiamen who thought that the Belgians were there to encourage their attack. The Belgians never made any use of armed T-6s though, then their pilots could usually not differentiate between 'friend' and 'foe'.
10. This sub-charter is based on Lefèvre, pp55-56, 91-154; Péries et all, pp117, 121-140; Prunier, *The Rwanda Crisis*, pp54-57; Rusugara, pp142-155 & de Brouwer
11. This sub-chapter is based on interview with Gasana, June 2014; Péries et all, pp141-146; Prunier; Lionet, *Resilience of a Nation*
12. Contrary to what was happening in so many other African states of the time, only one coup plot became known through all of the 1970s and 1980s. This was planned by two members of Habyarimana's inner circle – Col Alexis Kanyarengwe and Maj Théoneste Lizinde – but revealed on time because they did not have direct control over any of FAR units. Kanyarengwe was subsequently forced into exile, while Lizinde was arrested and jailed.
13. Habyarimana's Deputy CoS, Col Laurent Serubuga, served in this position without interruption from 1973 until 1991.
14. As such, units like the Mutara Independent Company were not 'secondary' by nature, but their standards were degraded because of described practices.
15. Except where mentioned otherwise, this sub-chapter is based on Lanotte; Morel; Thimonier; *Mission parlementaire sur le Rwanda*; Gacharuzi, *The Path of a Genocide*
16. Neretse, pp21-22; Péries et all, pp161-176
17. Ntabakuze, *Final Trial Brief*; *Ntabakuze Deposition*, September 2006 & *Réglement sur l'organisation de l'armée rwandaise*, MINADEF, November 1987
18. This sub-chapter is based on *Rapport de la mission de recco de l'ONU 1993*; Péries et all, pp166-174; Neretse, pp19, 51-52, 291 & Thimonier
19. This sub-chapter is based on Neretse, pp51-54; *Annex: Ntabakuze Deposition in September 2006*; *Situation officiers armée rwandaise*, MINADEF, 1 January 1993; *Reglement sur l'organisation de l'armée rwandaise*, November 1987
20. Total FAR manpower as of 1990 is difficult to assess, because various sources cite entirely different figures. For example, the army is usually said to have had anything between 5,200 and 8,600 troops – including 300 officers and 1,300 NCOs – in active service. Available trained reserve is usually assessed at about 1,500.
21. Exact size of the FAR's military police before the Rwandan Civil War of 1990-1994 remains unclear. It is possible that it consisted of a single company.
22. It remains unclear how many AMLs were acquired by Rwanda from France. 12 AML-60s were delivered in 1967, and 17 AML-90s in 1986, but other deliveries must have taken place then the Reconnaissance Battalion is known to have operated no less than 39 vehicles of both

variants as of 1992, despite losses it suffered during the first two years of the war.

23. This sub-chapter is based on Morel, pp93-96; Périès et all, pp163-176; Neretse, pp21, 51-54; *Situation officiers armée rwandaise*, MINADEF, 1 January 1993; *Situation officiers armée rwandaise*, MINADEF, 5 March 1994; *Compte-rendu trimestriel DMAT Air, Kigali*, 24 January 1991 & *TD Kigali 116*

24. France originally donated two Noratlas transports, in 1984 and 1986, registered 9XR-GX and 9XR-GY, respectively, but only one of these remained intact by 1990 and was used as source of spares for the other example.

25. Indeed, even the French called their COIN doctrine the 'revolutionary warfare'.

26. Prunier, The *Rwanda Crisis*, pp61-67; Prunier, 'Éléments pour une historie du Front patriotique rwandais' *(Politique Africaine,* Vol. XIII, No 51, 1993)*;* Clapham, pp119-133; Rusagara, pp168-171; Adelman et all, pp31-50; Missier; Heming, pp18-64; UNHCR, 'The State of the World's Refugees, 2000: Fifty Years of Humanitarian Action', pp47-52

27. For details see sister-publication from Africa@War series, Volume 23: *Wars and Insurgencies of Uganda, 1971-1994.*

28. Sources differ in regards of exact number of victims of UNLA's terror in Luweero Triangle, citing between 100.000 and 300.000 deaths.

29. It is likely that fresh memories of arduous sieges of Masaka and Mbarara were another reason for the NRA letting majority of Kampala garrison escape.

30. Kainerugaba, pp156-163, Museveni, pp160-168; note that most of 'battalions' in question were much larger than their designation might imply; some were in control of up to 1,900 combatants.

31. Kinzer, pp38-39

32. Ssemujju Ibrahim Nganda, 'Who fought: Kagame helped Museveni crush internal NRA revolt', *observer.ug*

33. Kinzer, pp39-40; Prunier, The Rwanda Crisis, pp67-71; Figures vary, with estimates ranging from 500 to between 3,000 and 4,000 Rwandans out of about 30,000 NRA fighters led by Museveni at the time he took Kampala.

34. Unless cited otherwise, this sub-chapter is based on Clapham, p107, 123-128; Prunier, 'Éléments pour une historie du Front patriotique rwandais' (Politique Africaine, Vol XIII, No. 51, 1993); Adelman et all, pp31-49; Lamwaka, 'The Peace Process in Northern Uganda, 1986-1990 (Accord No. 11, 2002); Ruzibiza, pp95-99

35. For details, see sister-publication from Africa@War series, Volume 23: *Wars and Insurgencies in Uganda, 1971-1994*

36. Person who used to live in Kampala as of 1986, interview provided on condition of anonymity, March 2013.

37. Kinzer, p51

38. Melvern, p54 & Kato, 'Fred Rwigyema: the Military Genious from Two Countries', newvision.co.ug

39. Prunier, 'Éléments pour une historie du Front patriotique rwandais' (Politique Africaine, Vol XIII, No. 51, 1993). RPF's eight-point programme cited:
Restoration of unity among Rwandans;
Defending the sovereignty of the country and ensuring the security of people and property;
Establishment of democratic leadership;
Promoting the economy based on the country's natural resources;
Promoting social welfare;
Elimination of corruption, favouritism and embezzlement of national resources;
Promoting international relations based on mutual respect, cooperation and mutually beneficial economic exchange.

40. Guichaoua

41. Otunnu

42. Adelman et all, pp31-49; *The Mukara Massacre of 1989*, Justice & Reconciliation Project, Field Note XII, March 2011

43. 'Perspective Monde' (University de Sherbrook, perspective. usherbrooke.ca)

44. Missier, pp10-55

45. Clapham, pp125-128; Prunier 'Éléments pour une historie du Front patriotique rwandais' (Politique Africaine, Vol XIII, No. 51, 1993)

46. RPF Constitution (http://rpfinkotanyi.org/wp/?page_id=97, 2008)

47. Rusegera, p175; curiously, such dancing teams were all named after traditional military formations from pre-colonial times.

48. Kato, 'Fred Rwigyema: the Military Genious from Two Countries', newvision.co.ug

49. Turner, p211. While countering the way in which French authorities and majority of French historians consider the situation in Africa, this 'purely ethnical' explanation is denied by proponents of other – foremost 'ideology-related' – perspectives. For example, there is a thesis that Museveni was exposed to and strongly influenced by progressive African nationalism already during his youth, and saw such leaders like Mobutu of Zaire and Habyarimana of Rwanda as 'mere agents of Western imperialism' without any legitimacy. If this was the case, it cannot be denied that once in power in Kampala, but especially while involving Uganda in the I and II Congo Wars (fought 1996-1997, and 1998-2003, respectively), Museveni was quick in siding with some of most important figures of precisely the same 'Western imperialism', foremost the USA, Great Britain, and Israel. Whether one prefers to accept the 'purely ethnical' or 'ideology related' variant, fact is that from the standpoint of several involved African statesmen, the 'purely ethnical' theory did play an important role not only in conflicts in Uganda and Rwanda, but also in the DRC. Best example for this was delivered during a conference of African leaders hosted by French President Jacques Chirac, in Paris, in 1998, when Laurent Kabila (President of the DRC, 1997-2001) had accused Museveni and Kagame of a hidden plot to build a Hima-Tutsi empire. Museveni interjected, saying the meeting should discuss more serious issues. Robert Mugabe (President of Zimbabwe) felt irritated by Museveni's talk of 'more serious issues' and insisted the threat of a Hima-Tutsi empire was a real and serious issue: 'I have always heard that you are a very intelligent and popular man,' Mugabe told Museveni right into his face. 'I now think your intelligence is quite exaggerated.' With that, Mugabe walked out of the meeting in protest, wagging his finger at Museveni and vowing to, 'fight to the death' against the, 'creation of a Hima-Tutsi empire' (see 'WikiLeaks: Dirtly Little Secrets out , Whistleblowing Site leaves many world leaders exposed', The Observer online, 18 September 2011).

50. Missier, p55

51. Kuperman, p7

52. Neretse, pp7 & 68; Ruzibiza, pp102-107

53. James Kabarebe, 'Rwanda Invasion: Kagame breathes life into collapsing struggle' (monitor.co.ug, 6 October 2013)

54. Faustin Mugabe, 'Rwanda Invasion : RPF Fires First Shot at Mirama Hills/Kagitumba Border', *Daily Monitor*, 17 March 2014 ; Editorial, 'RPF Invasion of Rwanda and Denials', *Daily Monitor*, 18 December 2012, Prunier, p132 & Embassy SITREP No.25 ('Confidential Kigali 04307'), from 25 October 1990

55. Kuperman, p8 & Rwigyema, interview to Fausto Biloslavo, January 1987. Notable is that during this interview, Rwigyema observed, 'Now Uganda, tomorrow Rwanda', indicating intention of Rwandan refugees fighting for the NRA to – 'sometimes in the future' – launch an invasion of their homeland. Furthermore, ever since October 1990, there are rumours circling within circles of Rwandan exiles (for example James Gasana, interview, June 2014), that Fred Rwigyema was secretly negotiating with Habyarimana. Accordingly, President of Rwanda intended to use this invasion as a pretext to enforce the idea

of a peaceful deal with insurgents within circles of his own supporters. Although never confirmed by any kind of evidence (even more so because both protagonists of these alleged negotiations have meanwhile died), such rumours sound reasonable considering recollections of his comrades about character and nature of Fred Rwigyema. Obviously, if the rumours in question are based on facts, the two leaders had entirely different plans for the future of their nation – and these stood in diagonal opposition to what eventually happened.

56. Editorial, 'RPF Invasion of Rwanda and Denials', *Daily Monitor*, 18 December 2012 & ; James Kabarebe, 'Rwanda Invasion: Kagame breathes life into collapsing struggle' (monitor.co.ug, 6 October 2013)

57. Kuperman, p9

58. Neretse, p68 & Ruzibiza, p110

59. Ruzibiza, p111; 'Invaders Consolidated Hold on Rwandan Territories – Government of Rwanda prepares for Second Offensive' & 'Border Attack against Rwanda – SITREP No. 4'

60. Neretse, p69 & Ruzibiza, pp111-112

61. Lugan, p57

62. Melven, p65

63. Mahoux, Philippe & Verhofstadt, Guy, 'Commission d'enquête parlementaire concernant les événements du Rwanda; Rapport fait au nom de la Commission d'enquête' (Bruxelles, Sénat de Belgique, Session, de 1997-1998); Lefèvre, p158

64. Prunier, The *Rwanda Crisis*, pp94

65. Noble Marara, 'Behind the Presidential Curtains, Un-Answered questions about the death of Gen Fred Rwigyema', *inyenyerinews.org*

66. James Kabarebe, 'Rwanda Invasion: Kagame breathes life into collapsing struggle' (monitor.co.ug, 6 October 2013)

67. Missier, p56; James Kabarebe, 'Rwanda Invasion: Kagame breathes life into collapsing struggle' (monitor.co.ug, 6 October 2013); Abdul, pp109-112; Ruzibiza, pp109-112

68. Prunier, pp100-101; Lanotte, p74 & Lefèvre, p157

69. Lefèvre, pp160-161; Lanotte (pp216-217) describes French strategy as that of preventing a RPA-victory while using military aid as leverage to pressure Habyarimana into introducing democratic reforms and finding a negotiated settlement of the conflict.

70. Lefèvre, p158; notably, while including the word 'Marine' in their designation, these units are no 'naval infantry' as understood in Great Britain or the USA, but part of the French Army.

71. Lugan, p61-64

72. Lefèvre, p167

73. Lanotte, p248-250. Indeed, the budget granted for Belgian military cooperation with Rwanda was increased from about 100 million Belgian Francs per year in 1990, to about 200 million in 1993.

74. Although temporarily ending in late November 1990, the practice of appointing a French officer to the FAR HQ was resumed intermittently, later during the war (see Brana et all, Vol. 1, p137)

75. 'Zaire Deploys a Second Parachute Battalion to Rwanda', *Defence Military Agency*, Paris, 6 October 1990; ; James Kabarebe, 'Rwanda Invasion: Kagame breathes life into collapsing struggle' (monitor.co.ug, 6 October 2013); Christian Lionet, 'La bataille de Gabiro' (grandslacs. wordpress.com, 12 October 1990). For full details on organisation and structure of the FAZ as of that time, see Africa@War Volume13, *Great Lakes Holocaust*.

76. Lionet, p69 & ; James Kabarebe, 'Rwanda Invasion: Kagame breathes life into collapsing struggle' (monitor.co.ug, 6 October 2013) & SITREP No.17; The latter report indicated that only a small contingent of Zairian troops remained in Rwandan capital. Nevertheless, it took them only a few days to grain themselves a dubious reputation for sexual harassment and thievery.

77. Ruzibiza, pp112-113

78. Christian Lionet, 'La bataille de Gabiro' (grandslacs.wordpress.com, 12 October 1990) & SITREP No. 20

79. Christian Lionet, 'La bataille de Gabiro' (grandslacs.wordpress.com, 12 October 1990), Neretse, p69 & SITREP No. 20

80. SITREP No. 24

81. Christian Lionet, 'La bataille de Gabiro' (grandslacs.wordpress.com, 12 October 1990) & SITREP No. 24

82. SITREP No. 14 & No. 17

83. SITREP No. 20

84. SITREP No. 24

85. Missier, pp57-58

86. Missier, p58 & SITREP No. 25. According to Prunier (in Rwanda Crisis, p94) and Ruzibiza (p117), Bunyenyezi and Bayingana should have actually been executed by the RPA for either shooting Rwigyema or because they opposed a take-over by Paul Kagame. Indeed, according to one of versions about their death, both were shot by Kagame.

87. SITREP No. 23, No. 24 & No. 26

88. Trip Report (US Embassy), 8 November 1990

89. D. M. A. T/Air, 'compte-rendu trimestriel', Kigali, 24 January 1991; Lionet, p86 & SITREP No. 37

90. SITREP No. 39

91. Missier, p59

92. Kinzer, pp70-80 & Ruzibiza, pp126-127

93. Ruzibiza, pp126-127; SITREP No. 30, SITREP No. 31 & SITREP No. 32

94. Prunier, *Rwanda Crisis*, p147; Neretse, p86

95. Clapham, p131; Prunier, *Rwanda Crisis*, p115

96. Missier, pp60-62; Prunier, *Rwanda Crisis*, p115-117 & Kinzer, p82

97. Kinzer, p82

98. Prunier, *Rwanda Crisis*, p119

99. Missier, p17 & Rutabana, p138

100. Clapham, p132; Adelman et all, p56; Prunier, *African Guerilla*, p132 & *Rwanda Crisis*, p117. It is ironic that the RPF managed to run recruiting campaigns not only in countries like Burundi and Uganda, ruled by friendly governments, or Tanzania, ruled by a neutral government, but even in Zaire – which was actually an ally of the government in Kigali. Indeed, providing a clear testimony of the central government deliquescence during the last years of rule of Mobutu Sese Seko, the RPA set up a training camp in Bibwe, in North Kivu (see Gacharuzi, p56)

101. Missier, p68 & Rutabana, pp109-125

102. Brana et all, Vol. I, p133

103. Kinzer, pp83-84

104. Gasana, interview, April 2014 & Brana et all, p137

105. Gasana, interview, April 2014 & Brana et all, p137

106. Prunier, *Rwanda Crisis*, p113

107. Gasana, p101

108. Lettre au Colonel Cussac, 'Object: Bilan de l'instruction du battalion CECODO (41° Bataillon), 2° et 3° compagnie'

109. Report of the UN Reconnaissance Mission to Rwanda, September 1993

110. Melvern, pp31-32 & 119; SITREP No. 30 & SITREP No. 32; HRWAP 'Arming Rwanda'

111. SITREP No. 32; SITREP No. 34 & SITREP No. 35; Melvern, p121 & Fruchart, p8

112. Lugan, p112; Melvern, pp32, 119 & 121; Fruchart, p9

113. Prunier, Rwanda Crisis, pp114 & 159; Melvern, p61

114. Based on 'Situation officiers armée rwandaise arrêtée au 01 janvier 1993'

115. Brana et all, p552 & Varret, 'Compte-rendu de mission au Rwanda et au Burundi, 8-14 mai 1992'

116. Brana et all, pp146-147; notable is hat the 1e RPIMA is – contrary to other Marine Infantry Parachute Regiments – considered a 'special force' type of asset and thus subordinated directly to the French Army's Chief-of-Staff

117. Brana et all, p152 & Varret, 'Compte-rendu de mission au Rwanda et au Burundi, 8-14 mai 1992'

118. Périès, p199

119. Maj Ntabakuze, 'Final Trial Brief' & 'Rapport du colonel Capodanno', 10 November 1992

120. De Vulpian et all, p74

121. Dupaquier, p64; notably, the RPA's radio communications were not voice encrypted, but carefully coded; French equipment and training made the FAR SIGINT unit in question capable of not only intercepting but also reading these in near real-time.

122. Kinzer, p88-89; Ruzibiza, p132

123. Rwandan Patriotic Front attack on Ruhengeri', Kinzer, p89; Lugan, p79

124. Ruzibiza, p138 & Dupaquier, p64

125. Ruzibiza, p135

126. James Kabarebe, 'Rwanda Invasion: Kagame breathes life into collapsing struggle' (monitor.co.ug, 6 October 2013); Rutabana, p137

127. Ruzibiza, p147

128. Ibid, p148; Kinzer, pp91-96 & 120

129. Ruzibiza, pp152, 162-164; Péan, p109; Périès et all, p204

130. Neretse, p72; Lugan, p101 & Ruzibiza, p165

131. Lugan, p102 & Gasana, interview, April 2014

132. Ruzibiza, pp165-167; Rutabana, p145; interview with former RPA insurgent, provided on condition of anonymity, November 2014

133. Kuperman, p11; Lugan, p103; Neretse, p202

134. Gasana, interview, April 2014

135. Rapport du Colonel Capodanno sur sa mission au Rwanda, 10 November 1992

136. Gasana, interview, April 2014 & Guichaoua, p143

137. Prunier, *Rwanda Crisis*, pp136-138

138. Prunier, *Rwanda Crisis*, p175, Gaichaoua, p135

139. HRW, 'The Rwandan Patriotic Front' (in 'Leave None to Tell the Story: Genocide in Rwanda'); Ruzibiza, p209

140. Pruiner, *Rwanda Crisis*, p174; whether Kagame and his lieutenants were planning to seize Kigali and topple the government already at this stage, remains unclear.

141. Note that while the RPA should never have established more than eight 'Mobiles' existent as of 1993, but only continued expanding these, some sources (for example Gasana) indicate existence of between 20 and 30 CMFs of the RPA as of mid-1992. Like in the case of the NRA of 1986-1987 period, such organisation was providing the advantage of better coordination of larger number of men by the relatively small number of experienced officers.

142. Prunier, *Rwanda Crisis,* p132; Ruzibiza, pp185-186 & 189-192

143. Ruzibiza, p185

144. Gasana, interview, April 2014; Ruzibiza, p190, Lugan, p122; Neretse, pp73-74 & Tauzin, p61

145. Ruzibiza, p187 & Lugan, p122-123

146. Ruzibiza, p192 & Tauzin, p74

147. Lugan, p124-126

148. Tauzin, p68

149. Ibid, pp71 & 76

150. Ibid, p72, 76 & 78

151. Tauzin, p78 & Ruzibiza, p195

152. Dallaire, p102; Lugan, p122; Lanotte, p100

153. Dellaire, pp42 & 95

154. Castonguey, pp30-32 & 43

155. Castonguey, p44

156. Dellaire, p203; 'The Rwandan Patriotic Front' (in 'Leave None to Tell the Story: Genocide in Rwanda'); Kinzer, p130, Castonguey, pp90-91

157. Castonguey, pp47-48 & 53

158. Dallaire, pp181 & 215; Lefèvre, p177; Castonguey, pp65-66; only three of Belgian armoured vehicles were made operational by 21 Feburary 1994.

159. Dallaire, pp124, 152 & 177; Lanotte, pp122 & 133

160. Castonguey, p53; Lefèvre, pp176 & 180-181; Lanotte, p122

161. Dallaire, pp126-130; Ruzibiza, p212; Lefèvre, p179; Rutabana, p163 & Lanotte, p115

162. Castonguey, p53

163. Dallaire, pp166, 191-193; Castonguey, p79

164. Reyentjens, p15; Prunier, *Rwanda Crisis*, pp122-125 & 128; Guichaoua, p85

165. Gasana, interview, June 2014; Prunier, *Rwanda Crisis,* pp122-123; Reyentjens, p15

166. Guichaoua, pp149-150 & 167-171

167. Ibid, p135

168. Lanotte, p82; Guichaoua, pp159 & 212

169. Laffin, pp83-84 & Lanotte, p108

170. Dallaire, p114

171. Reyentjens, p16

172. Lanotte, p271-275

173. Guichaoua, pp305 & 341; Castonguey, p147 & Lanotte, p283

174. Contrary to statements by several contemporary sources, the officers in question never established something like a 'Crisis Committee' that would act as a sort of 'shadow government'.

175. Guichaoua, pp283 & 322; Prunier, *Rwanda Crisis*, p232

176. Neretse, p160

177. Melvern, pp139 & 146-147; Prunier, *Rwanda Crisis*, p229

178. Lanotte, pp283-284 & 289; Reyntjens, p126; Guichaoua, pp433-436; in comparison, the succeeding RPF government insists that 1,071,000 were killed, only 10% of them Hutu (see Rwanda, 'No consensus on genocide death toll', *AFP*, 6 April 2004). On the contrary, there are meanwhile several foreign, independent researchers who concluded that the conventional picture of the genocide is only partially correct. Accordingly, the RPF was clearly responsible for another major portion of the killings; the victims were fairly evenly distributed between Tutsi and Hutu; and another major portion of casualties were caused by 'unorganized' killings (that is murders committed for a large variety of other reasons by individuals that took profit from the utter chaos that engulfed the country). According to researchers in question, the majority of the dead were actually Hutu, rather than Tutsi – if for no other reason then because there were not enough Tutsi to find and murder. Furthermore, at some point in time anybody unable to prove he was Hutu by showing an identity card was killed on the spot by militiamen. Notable is that authors of most of such reports have been seriously threatened by members of the RPF government and – despite their repeated and explicit statements acknowledging the genocide of the Tutsis – labelled 'genocide deniers' (see Davenport et all, 'What Really Happened in Rwanda', psmag.com, 6 October 2009 & Reyntjens, p126)

179. Prunier, *Rwanda Crisis*, p249

180. De Vulpian et all, pp139-142 & 347; Prunier, *Rwanda Crisis*, p360; Reyntjens, p126; Guichaoua, p437 & HRW, 'The Rwandan Patriotic Front' (in 'Leave None to Tell the Story: Genocide in Rwanda'); Reyntjens, p126; notably, leaning on the famous *Gersony Report*, some sources cite 25,000 victims of RPA's atrocities during this period, but neither Gersony Report nor any other of available sources are citing any precise figures.

181. Castonguey, pp106, 111-113 & 116; Lefèvre, pp187-188 & Dallaire, pp239-241

182. Lefèvre, p195; Lanote, pp286-287; Castonguey, pp169-171. Notable is that the US and British representatives to the UN intensively lobbied for the end of the UNAMIR, contrary to French demands for the mission to be reinforced. Indeed, the US Ambassador to the UN, Madeleine Albraight, vetoed

183. Lugan, pp176-178; Thierry Charlier, 'Le sauvetage des ressortissants

occidentaux au Rwanda', Raids, Vol. 97 (June 1994); Romain Lefebvre, 'L'opération Amaryllis au Rwanda', Terre, Vol. 55 (June 1994); notably, the AdA deployed a total of eight C.160s and one C-130 in support of this operation.

184. Castonguey,p150; Lugan p178

185. *Los Angeles Times*, 10 April 1994

186. Lefèvre, p193; *Los Angeles Times*, 10 April 1994, Castonguey, p151

187. Neretse, p160 & Lanotre, p316

188. Neretse, p162; Lanotte, p321; Dallaire, p156; Lugan, p201; Fruchart/ SIPRI, 2007, pp14-15; according to Dallaire, the last aircraft to attempt landing at Kigali with a shipment of artillery- and mortar ammunition, a Douglas DC-8 transport, was captured by the UNAMIR troops and its load confiscated.

189. Ntikilina, p49 & Defence Intelligence Report, 9 May 1994

190. According to the RPF/RPA leadership, these preparations were 'mere contingency planning in case of a break-down of the Arusha Treaty by Habyarimana' (see Kinzer, p108).

191. Dellaire, pp200-201 & Ruzibiza, p251

192. Périès et all, pp291, 324, 348-350; Defence Intelligence Report, 9 May 1994. Notable was that many of fresh RPA recruits were Tutsi from the eastern DRC – including those settled there already by Belgians in the early 20th Century. Hundreds of them were trained and rushed to RPA units during the spring of that year. Although many lost their lives in subsequent fighting, dozens survived: some continued quite successful careers with the Rwandan military while others subsequently played a prominent role in various of insurgencies and mutinies inside the DRC of the 1990s and afterwards (for details, see *Africa@War* Volumes 13 and 14).

193. Lanotte, p315

194. Missier, p18; Debay, 'L'opération Tuquoise au Rwanda', Raids, No 101 (October 1994); Lanotte, p320

195. Dallaire, p228; Ntilikina, pp62-63

196. Dallaire, pp263-264; Ntikilina, pp67-69

197. Dallaire, p288; Ntikilina, pp69

198. It is unknown if the weapon in question was a ZPU-4 quad machine gun calibre 14.5mm or a Type-55 twin-barrel anti-aircraft cannon calibre 37mm.

199. Ntikilina, pp71-72 & 77; Ruzibiza, p264

200. Ruzibiza, pp284 & 292; Dallaire, p269

201. Ruzibiza, pp255-256; Dallaire, p291; Ruzibiza, p269

202. Ruzibiza, pp269-271 & 283; Ntikilina, p78

203. Ruzibiza, pp270-271

204. Dallaire, pp269 & 288; Ruzibiza, p256; Neretse, p161

205. Ruzibiza, pp287-290

206. Neretse, p161; Ruzibiza, p282 & Ntikilina, p78

207. Dallaire, p291, Ntikilina, pp72-73 & 77; Ruzibiza, pp260 & 264

208. Ntikilina, pp76-78; Dlaire, p334

209. Ntikilina, p79 & Dallaire, p341

210. Ruzibiza, p297; Ntikilina, p79; Dallaire, p353 & Ruzibiza, p292

211. Ntikilina, pp79-80; Ruzibiza, pp297-298

212. Rutabana, p180

213. Dallaire, pp299 & 378; Ruzibiza, pp295-296

214. Ntikilina, pp83-86M; Dallaire, p421

215. Ntikilina, pp86-87

216. Ntikilina, p87; Missier, p18

217. Ruzibiza, pp300-301

218. Ruzibiza, pp301-304 & 315-316; Dallaire, p410; Missier, p18

219. Ntikilina, pp99-100

220. Ruzibiza, pp319-320 & 324-326; Ntikilina, p110

221. Prunier, *Rwanda Crisis*, p299

222. Odom, p89

223. Lanotte, p481 & Prunier, p312

224. Lanotte, p384 & Castonguey, p177

225. Lanotte, pp419-422

226. Aged and ill, Mitterrand did not intend to candidate for next elections, but most of members of his government – which was a coalition of two different conservative parties – did.

227. Ibid, pp477-479

228. Debay, 'L'opération Turquoise au Rwanda', *Raids*, No. 101 (October 1994)

229. Lanotte, pp429-430; Prunier, p291

230. Lugan, p214

231. Lanotte, pp429-435; 'Zone Turquoise' was actually an unofficial designation; official variant could be translated as the 'Secure Humanitarian Area' (SHA) – the concept of which was closely related to experiences from UN operations in Bosnia i Herzegovina.

232. Lanotte, p432; Debay, 'L'opération Turquoise au Rwanda', *Raids*, No. 101 (October 1994)

233. Debay, 'L'opération Turquoise au Rwanda', *Raids*, No. 101 (October 1994)& Lugan, p223

234. Lanotte, pp416-417

235. Lanotte, pp405 & 435; Lugan, pp239-240; Silence Turquoise, p335; Tauzin, p138

236. Tauzin, pp141-143 & Lugan, p222

237. Debay, Debay, 'L'opération Turquoise au Rwanda', Raids, No. 101 (October 1994); notably, although the Operation Turquoise was closely covered by the media, Debay was the only one to report about this clash between the RICM and the RPA. Born in former Belgian-Congo, and having served in the former armed forces of Rhodesia, Debay became a journalist specialised in reporting about military affairs. During his 30-years-long career – which ended with his tragic death in Aleppo, in Syria, in January 2013 – he developed intimate knowledge about French armed forces, and was thus in a far better position to report about their operations than any 'mainstream' media journalists. Because of this, his reporting about RCIM-RPA clash can be trusted. For Debay's biography, see Rémy Ourdan, 'Yves Debay, fou de guerre et aventurier iconoclaste', *le monde online*, 14 February 2013

238. Lanotte, p427; according to Col William Bagire (CO 7th Mobile), the RPA mortars were trying to hit Mount Goma to prevent retreating FAR units from positioning their artillery pieces there. However, his shells fell near the airport because the mortar-crew s had difficulties estimating the range (see Odom, p91)

239. Lanotte, pp435, 444 & 481; notably, in reaction to this epidemics, the USA launched the 'Operation Support Hope' with the aim of airlifting water and food to Goma and Kigali in order to stabilise the situation in refugee camps.

240. Ever since, French involvement in Rwanda – and especially Operation Turquoise – are a subject of often fierce polemics and debate in France. One of reasons is that the French units deployed in Rwanda re-armed around 40 Rwandan Gendarmes in order to establish a small, local law-enforcement capability. In turn, this is often presented as a proof of support for genocidal Rwandan government. Something similar can be said about the case of a group of Tutsi survivors of the Bisesero massacre found by a small patrol of French special-forces operatives early during this operation: the French troops had to let the survivors go because they lacked numbers and capability to properly protect them. By the time reinforcements arrived, three days later, Hutu extremists slaughtered additional victims. Some of French activists explain this tragedy as a more or less 'deliberate' complicity of the French military that, according to them, had purposely allowed its 'Interhamwe allies' to 'finish the job' (see Lugan, pp257, 261-262 & 270; Lanotte, pp465, 471)

241. *Gersony Report*; Reyntjens, p126; Prunier, *Africa's World War*, p16; Cooper, *Great Lakes Holocaust & Great Lakes Conflagration*

Selected Bibliography

While researching for this project, the authors have found a host of information of purely military nature, but scattered over a myriad of sources. For reasons of space, we could not entirely follow the academic referencing pattern; indeed, we could not even list all the sources of reference we have used. Even so, we feel there is a need to forewarn the reader that we found ourselves without solution but to make use of controversial-, and sources sometimes heavily biased toward specific, often dubious agendas – but still providing valuable information related to military affairs. Not only that the information provided by such sources was carefully cross-examined, but we would like to stress that opinions expressed in certain of works in question should by no means be misunderstood as 'endorsed' by the authors.

Adelman, Howard & Suhrke, Astri (editors), *The Path of a Genocide: The Rwanda Crisis from Uganda to Zaire*, (New Brunswick, Transaction Publishers, 1999), ISBN 91-7106-432-X

Braeckman, Colette, *Rwanda: Histoire d'un génocide*, (Fayard, 1996), ISBN 2-213-59356-6

Brana, Pierre & Cazeneuve, Bernard, *Enquête sur la tragédie rwandaise: Rapport d'information déposé par la Mission d'information de la Commission de la Défense nationale et des Forces armées et de la Commission des Affaires étrangères sur les opérations militaires menées par la France, d'autres pays et l'ONU au Rwanda entre 1990 et 1994, T.I (Rapport), T.II (Annexes), T.III/1 & 2 (Auditions)*, (Paris : Assemblée nationale, number 1271, December 1998), online version

Castonguay, Jacques, *Les Casques bleus au Rwanda*, (L'Harmattan, 1998), ISBN 2-7384-6472-6

Charlier, Thierry, 'Operation Green Been pour les Paras-Codos', Raids No 56 (January 1991)

Charlier, Thierry, 'Le sauvetage des ressortissants occidentaux au Rwanda', *Raids* No 97 (June 1994)

Chrétien, Jean-Pierre, *L'Afrique des Grands Lacs : Deux mille ans d'histoire*, (Paris, Aubier, 2000), ISBN 2-70-072294-9

Clapham, Christopher (Editor), *African Guerrillas: Eritrea/Tigray/Sudan/Somalia/Uganda/Rwanda/Congo-Zaire/Liberia/Sierra Leone*, (Oxford, James Currey Ltd, 1998), ISBN 0-85255-815-5

Cooper, Tom & Weinert, Peter, with Hinz, Fabian & Lepko Mark, *African MiGs Vol. 2: -Madagascar to Zimbabwe - MiGs and Sukhois in Service in Sub-Saharan Africa*, (Harpia Publishing, L.L.C, 2011), ISBN 978-0-9825539-8-5

Dallaire, Roméo, *Shake Hands with the Devil: The failure of Humanity in Rwanda*, (Da Capo Press, 2005), ISBN 978-0-7867-1510-7

De Brouwer, Wilfried, Le journal d'un Pilote FAF: Congo/Ruanda-Urundi 1960/1961, (*vieillestiges.be*, 15 December 2007)

De Vulpain, Laure & Prungnaud, Thierry, *Silence Turquoise: Rwanda, 1992-1994, Responsabilités de l'État français dans le génocide des Tutsi*, (Don Quichotte éditions, 2012), ISBN 978-2-35949-092-3

Debay, Yves, L'opération 'Turquoise' au Rwanda, *Raids* No. 101, Octobre 1994

Dupaquier, Jean-François, *L'agenda du génocide: Le témoignage de Richard Mugenzi ex-espion rwandais* (Éditions Karthala, 2010), ISBN 978-2-8111-0413-9

Duruz, Grégoire, *Par-delà le Génocide: Dix-sept récits contre l'effacement de l'histoire au Rwanda* (Yvelineéditions, 2014), ISBN 978-2-84668-467-5

Fruchart, Damien, *United Nations Arms Embargoes: Their Impact on Arms Flows and Target Behaviour. Case Study : Rwanda, 1994-present* (Stockholm International Peace Research Institute, 2007)

Gasana, James K, *Rwanda: du parti-Etat à l'État-garnison*, (L'Harmattan, 2002), ISBN 978-2-74751-317-3

Gerstenzang, James, 'Marines on Alert as Americans Flee Rwanda Fighting' (Los Angeles Times, 10 April 1994, via articles.latimes.com)

Gréa, Alain, 'Les Grises exotiques', (*escadrilles.org*)

Griswold, Eliza, The Man for a New Sudan, (The New York Times, 15 June 2008)

Guichaoua, André, *Rwanda: De la guerre au Génocide, les politiques criminelles au Rwanda (1990-1994)*, (Paris, Éditions La Découverte, 2010), ISBN 978-2-7071-5370-8

Heming, Alexa, Fighting Their Way Home: The Militarization of the Rwandan '59ers, (thesis, University of Cape Town, 2007)

Human Rights Watch, *Leave None to Tell the Story: Genocide in Rwanda* (online version)

Human Rights Watch Arms Project, Arming Rwanda: *The Arms Trade and Human Rights Abuses in the Rwandan War*, January 1994

Jackson, Peter Drake, *French Ground Force organisational Development for counterrevolutionary warfare between 1945 and 1962*, (thesis, US Army Command and General Staff College, Fort Leavenworth, 2005)

Kabarebe, James, 'Rwanda Invasion: Kagame breathes life into collapsing struggle' (*monitor.co.ug*, 6 October 2013)

Kainerugaba, Muhoozi, *Battles of the Ugandan Resistance. A Tradition of Maneuver* (Kampala: Fountain Publishers, 2010) ISBN 978-9970-25-032-5

Kalyegira, Timothy, '30 years after the fall of Amin, causes of 1979 war revealed' (*monitor.co.ug*, 11 April 2009)

Kasfir, Nelson, *Dilemmas of Popular Support in Guerrilla War: The National Resistance Army in Uganda, 1981-1986* (First Draft, Dartmouth College, 2002)

Kato, Joshua, 'Fred Rwigyema, the military genius from two countries', (newvision.co.ug, 10 April 2012)

Kinzer, Stephen, *A Thousand Hills: Rwanda's Rebirth and the Man Who Dreamed It*, (Hoboken, John Wiley & Sons, Inc, 2008), ISBN 978-0-470-12015-6

Kuperman, Alan J, *Explaining the Ultimate Escalation in Rwanda: How and Why Tutsi Rebels Provoked a Retaliatory Genocide*, 2003 (draft of the article 'Post-Genocide Rwanda: Ten Years Later', from March 2004, planned for publication in a special issue of the Journal of Genocide Research)

Lamwaka, Caroline, *The peace process in northern Uganda, 1986-1990* (Accord No. 11, 2002)

Lanotte, Olivier, *La France au Rwanda (1990-1994): Entre abstention impossible et engagement ambivalent*, (Bruxelles, P.I.E Peter Lang, 2007), ISBN 978-90-5201-344-2

Lefevre, Romain, 'L'opération Amaryllis au Rwanda', *Terre*, Vol. 55 (June 1994)

Lefèvre, Patrick & Lefèvre, Jean-Noël, *Les militaires belges et le Rwanda 1916-2006*, (Bruxelles, Éditions Racines, 2006), ISBN 978-2-87386-489-7

Laffin, John, *The World in Conflict: Contemporary Warfare Described and Analysed* (Herndon, Brassey's Inc., 1996) ISBN 1-85753-196-5

Lionet, Christian, 'La bataille de Gabiro' (*grandslacs.wordpress.com*)

Lugan, Bernard, *François Mitterrand, l'armée française et le Rwanda*, (Éditions du Rocher, 2005), ISBN 2 268 05 060 2

Mahoux, Philippe & Verhofstadt, Guy, *Commission d'enquête parlementaire concernant les événements du Rwanda. Rapport fait au nom de la Commission d'enquête*, (Bruxelles:Sénat de Belgique, Session de 1997-1998)

Manea, Octavian, 'Reflections on the French School of Counter-Rebellion: An Interview with Etienne de Durand', (*SmallWarsJournal.com*, 3 March, 2011)

Marara, Noble, 'Behind the Presidential Curtains: Un-answered questions about the death of Gen Fred Rwigema', (inyenyerinews.org)

Melvern, Linda, *Complicités de génocide : comment le monde a trahi le Rwanda*, (Paris, Karthala, 2010), ISBN 9782811103637

Misser, François, *Vers un nouveau Rwanda ? Entretiens avec Paul Kagamé*, (Karthala, 1995), ISBN 2-86537-598-6

Morel, Jacques, *La France au coeur du génocide des Tutsi*, (L'Esprit Frappeur & Izuba), ISBN 978-2-84405-242-1

Mugabe, Faustin, 'How Amin tracked Fronasa rebels', (monitor.co.ug, 10 February 2013), consulted 8 February 2014

Mugabe, Faustin, 'Rwanda Invasion: RPF fires first shot at Mirama Hills/Kagitumba border' (*monitor.co.ug*, 1 October 2013)

Musinguzi, Bamuturaki, 'Lies drove Amin to strike Tanzania', (*monitor.co.ug*, 25 November 2012)

Neretse, Emmanuel, *Grandeur et décadence des Forces Armées Rwandaises*, (Lille, Editions Sources du Nil, 2010), ISBN 2-9521712-8-9

Nganda, Ssemujju Ibrahim, Who Fought?: 10 brave men who faced UNLA's fire, (*observer.ug*, 18 June 2009)

Nganda, Ssemujju Ibrahim, Who Fought?: How Kyaligonza terrorised Kampala, (*observer.ug*, 24 June 2009)

Nganda, Ssemujju Ibrahim, Who Fought?: Kagame helped Museveni Crush internal NRA revolt, (online article, *observer.ug*, 6 August 2009)

Ntilikina, Faustin, *Rwanda: La prise de Kigali et la chasse aux réfugiés par l'Armée du Général Paul Kagame*, (Lille, Editions Sources du Nile, 2008), ISBN 2-9521712-5-4

Odom, Thomas, P., *Journey into Darkness: Genocide in Rwanda* (Texas A&M University Press, 2005) ISBN 1-58544-427-8

Omara-Otunnu, Amii, *Politics and the Military in Uganda, 1890-1985*, (Basingstoke, The MacMillan Press Ltd, 1987), ISBN 0-333-41980-4

Péan, Pierre, *Noirs fureurs, blancs menteurs*, (Paris, Éditions Mille et une nuits, 2005), ISBN 2-842-05629-8

Périès, Gabriel & Servenay, David, *Une guerre noire: Enquête sur les origines du génocide rwandais (1959-1994)*, Éditions La Découverte, Paris, 2007, ISBN 978-2-7071-4914-5

Prunier, Gérard & Calas, Bernard, *L'Ouganda contemporain*, (Karthala, Paris, 1994), ISBN 978-2865-37-471-7

Prunier, Gérard, Éléments pour une histoire du Front patriotique rwandais, (*Politique Africaine*, No. 51, 1993)

Prunier, Gérard, 'Le phénomène NRM en Ouganda'. Une expérience révolutionnaire originale, (*Politique Africaine*, No 23, septembre 1986)

Prunier, Gerard, *The Rwanda Crisis: History of a Genocide*, (London, Hurst & Company, 1997), ISBN 978-1-85065-372-1

Reyntjens, Filip, *Rwanda:Gouverner après le génocide*, (Paris, les belles lettres, 2014), ISBN 978-2-251-44492-5

Ringquist, John & Thomas, Charles, *Jeshi la Wananchi la, The Tanzanian Military, Social Change, and Structural Resiliency: A Network Science Approach*, (Network Science Center at West Point, November 2011)

Rusagara, Frank K, *Resilience of a Nation: A History of the Military in Rwanda*, (Kigali, Fountain Publishers, 2009), ISBN 978-9970-19-001-0

Rutabana, Benjamin, *De l'enfer à l'enfer : Du Hutu Power à la dictature de Kagame*, (Books Éditions, 2014), ISBN 978-2-36608-045-2

Ruzibiza, Abdul Joshua, *Rwanda: l'histoire secrète*, (Paris, Éditions du Panama, 2005), ISBN 2-7557-0093-9

Sengooba, Nicholas, 'Milton Obote is the most influential Ugandan in our 50-year history', (monitor.co.ug, 9 October 2012)

Tauzin, Didier, *Rwanda: Je demande justice pour la France et ses soldats*, (Éditions Jacob-Duvernet , 2011), ISBN 978-2-84724-335-2

Thimonier, Olivier, *La politique de la France au Rwanda de 1960 à 1981*, (mémoire de maîtrise, Paris, Université Paris I Panthéon-La Sorbonne, 2001)

Waugh, Colin M, *Paul Kagame and Rwanda: Power, Genocide and the Rwandan Patriotic Front*, (Mcfarland & Co Inc Pub, 2004), ISBN 978-1-4766-1315-4

Much of the additional information was obtained in the course of interviews with various participants (see Acknowledgements), and online archives like francerwandagenocide.org and rwandadocumentsproject.net, between November 2013 and April 2014. Sadly, the exhaustive archive of the latter website is not available online any more. Additional online sources of reference included websites like cia.gov, perspective.usherbrooke.ca, worldmilitair.com, unhcr.org, air-britain.com, The Library of Congress Country Studies, gaf.mil.gh, uca.edu (University of Central Arkansas), gwu.edu (The George Washington University), and arts.ubc.ca (The University of British Columbia).

Acknowledgements

Projects of this kind are always a matter of lots of networking and indeed, teamwork. The authors relied greatly on cooperation with a number of individuals from around the world, who greatly helped collect relevant information and photographs. Our gratitude is therefore due to a number of persons, starting with James K Gasana (former Minister of Defence of Rwanda), who not only granted us plenty of his precious time to patiently answer all our questions, but also provided insight and knowledge that are well beyond invaluable. Fausto Biloslavo from Italy kindly provided his experience from trips to Uganda and many of photographs he has taken there; Albert Grandolini from France shared many photographs from his extensive collection, or otherwise helped establish contacts to sources of information and photographs; and Gérard Colom from France who shared photographs from his collection.

Last but not least, we would like to express our gratitude to our wives, for always patiently accompanying us, at all the times providing the support required to complete our research and 'put it to paper'.

Authors

Tom Cooper

Tom Cooper, from Austria, is a military-aviation journalist and historian. Following a career in worldwide transportation business – in which, during his extensive travels in Europe and the Middle East, he established excellent contacts – he moved into writing. An earlier fascination with post-Second World War military aviation has narrowed to focus on smaller air forces and conflicts, about which he has collected extensive archives of material. Concentrating primarily on air warfare that has previously received scant attention, he specialises in investigative research on little-known African and Arab air forces, as wella s the Iranian air force. Cooper has published 23 books – including the unique 'Arab MiGs' series, which examined the development and service history of major Arab air forces in conflicts with Israel – as well as over 250 articles on related topics, providing a window into a number of previously unexamined yet fascinating conflicts and relevant developments.

Adrien Fontanellaz

Adrien Fontanellaz, from Switzerland, is a military history researcher and author. He developed a passion for military history at an early age and has progressively narrowed his studies to modern-day conflicts. He is a member of the Scientific Committee of the Pully-based Centre d'histoire et de prospective militaires (Military History and Prospective Centre), and regularly contributing articles for the *Revue Militaire Suisse* and various French military history magazines. He is co-founder and a regular contributor to the the French military history website *L'autre côté de la colline*.